91

PSALM

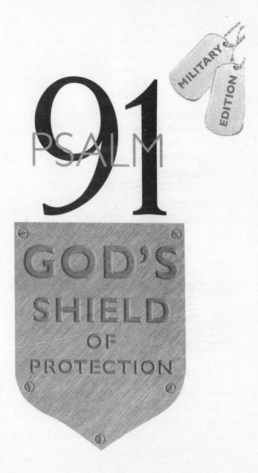

GOD'S
SHIELD
OF
PROTECTION

PEGGY JOYCE RUTH
ANGELIA RUTH SCHUM

Psalm 91
God's Shield of Protection
Copyright © 2005, 2007, 2009
Peggy Joyce Ruth BETTER LIVING Ministries
www.peggyjoyceruth.org
All rights reserved.

Scripture quotations are from the *New American Standard Bible* (NASB)* 1960, 1977, 1995 by the Lockman Foundation. Used by permission.
The Holy Bible, King James Version (KJV)
The Holy Bible, New International Version (NIV)* 1973, 1984 by International Bible Society, used by permission of Zondervan Publishing House
The Amplified Bible (AMP)* 1965, 1987 by Zondervan Publishing House

First Printing, 2007
Printed in the United States of America
Cover and interior design by Standing Pixels

This book made available without charge by The 1687 Foundation, a nonprofit, tax-exempt organization dedicated to advancing spiritual and charitable purposes. Please note that these books may only be given away. They cannot be sold, cannot be used to raise money, and cannot be a "free giveaway" for any commercial or personal-gain purpose whatsoever.

For additional information, please contact:
Email: info@1687foundation.com
Tel: 541.549.7600
Fax: 541.549.7603

Ever since I was introduced to Peggy Joyce's *Psalm 91* I have made it my personal mission to get this book into the hands of as many soldiers as possible. Because I work for the Army I am acutely aware of the dangers that our men and women face on a daily basis. God's ultimate umbrella of protection has become a daily prayer for me and many of our deployed troops. It is my sincere hope that we can flood the theater of operations with this phenomenal book.

—**Jo Anne Cyr,** Department of the Army Civilian

If your ears have become dull to God's promises, get *Psalm 91: God's Shield of Protection*, by Peggy Joyce Ruth, and be renewed to a heart of faith in God's provision of protection. My family has received great and tangible comfort from Psalm 91, and Peggy Joyce's book was the catalyst.

—**Captain Hank Bond,** U.S. Navy

Peggy Joyce Ruth's masterpiece, *Psalm 91: God's Shield of Protection,* captivates the attention of anyone needing salvation, comfort, healing, protection, or encouragement.

—**James F. Linzey, D.D.,** Chaplain, Major, USA

Psalm 91: God's Shield of Protection is a well-done, timely message of the precious promise of God that has sustained America's troops in times of conflict down through the ages.

—**Colonel E. H. Jim Ammerman** (Ret.)

Peggy Joyce Ruth's book, *Psalm 91: God's Shield of Protection,* explains those promises in such an enlightening way that everyone can rest in His protection and focus on his own mission.

—**Lt. Colonel Michael D. Melendez,** U.S. Army

Peggy Joyce has done it again. Your faith will grow as you read Peggy Joyce's interpretation of Psalm 91 and hear these glorious testimonies!

—**Scott Kennedy,** Operation Prayer Shield

Psalm 91

He who dwells in the shelter of the Most High
Will abide in the shadow of the Almighty.
I will say to the LORD, "My refuge and my fortress,
My God, in whom I trust!"
For it is He who delivers you
from the snare of the trapper
And from the deadly pestilence.
He will cover you with His pinions,
And under His wings you may seek refuge;
His faithfulness is a shield and bulwark.

You will not be afraid of the terror by night,
Or of the arrow that flies by day;
Of the pestilence that stalks in darkness,
Or of the destruction that lays waste at noon.
A thousand may fall at your side,
And ten thousand at your right hand,
But it shall not approach you.
You will only look on with your eyes
And see the recompense of the wicked.
For you have made the LORD, my refuge,
Even the Most High, your dwelling place.

No evil will befall you,

Nor will any plague come near your tent.

For He will give His angels charge concerning you,

To guard you in all your ways.

They will bear you up in their hands,

That you do not strike your foot against a stone.

You will tread upon the lion and cobra,

The young lion and the serpent

you will trample down.

"Because he has loved Me,

therefore I will deliver him;

I will set him securely on high,

Because he has known My name.

"He will call upon Me, and I will answer him;

I will be with him in trouble;

I will rescue him, and honor him.

"With a long life I will satisfy him

And let him behold My salvation."

Contents

Foreword

General George C. Marshall, U.S. Army Chief of Staff during World War II, once said, "We are building… morale, not on supreme confidence in our ability to conquer and subdue other peoples; not in reliance on things of steel and the super-excellence of guns and planes and bombsights, but on things more potent. We are building it on *belief;* for it is what men *believe* that makes them invincible."[1]

During my experience as a chaplain to a battalion of U.S. Marines in Iraq, I saw firsthand what happens when belief in Almighty God floods the hearts and souls of men and women rushing into the teeth of battle. This supreme confidence in God is not foxhole religion or superficial faith—it is a life-changing decision to place oneself in the loving hands of Him who is greater than the battlefield.

Such a faith is nowhere more vividly demonstrated than in the words of Psalm 91. For thousands of years the "Soldier's Psalm" has given warriors a reservoir of truth to draw from when the night is dark and the task is difficult. In this timely companion to this timeless psalm, Peggy Joyce Ruth has made clear and accessible the power of God's promises to those who face the ruination and rubble of war.

For those on the home front, read this book as a practical guide to radical intercessory prayer on behalf of your marine, sailor, soldier, or airman.

For those heroes on the front lines, read this book for strength, hope, courage, and salvation. And as you walk with God through the valley of the shadow of death, may the awesome power of His promises, shared in this book, fill your heart, rule your mind, and shield your life.

For "He who dwells in the shelter of the Most High will abide in the shadow of the Almighty" (Psalm 91:1).

—LT Carey H. Cash; Chaplain, USN
Chaplain to the President

Introduction

Nothing could have thrilled my heart more than what recently took place in our hometown. The men and women of the National Guard, along with their families, had just been honored with a citywide dinner, featuring patriotic speeches and lengthy goodbyes. In the midst of all the commotion, I piled stacks of my Psalm 91 books on my portable card table and attempted to place one with each of the military personnel, for themselves and their families. Yet as determined as I was, all evening long I wondered how many of the books would be misplaced, laid down, or forgotten in all the excitement.

I have a father who served in WWII, a brother and a brother-in-law who each served in the military, and a grandson who is now an Air Force policeman. No wonder my heart ached to have our soldiers see the awesome protection covenant from God that is brought to light in this book! But I doubted that they'd pay much attention to what had been pushed into their hands during all the celebration.

However, as the military buses carrying them to their deployment passed—to my absolute delight and in response to a homemade sign held up by the cheering crowd, bearing the words, *"We are praying Psalm 91 for you!"*—several of the guys in uniform held their copies of *Psalm 91: God's Umbrella of Protection* out the bus windows as they drove by.

What a relief to know that God was already working behind the scenes. They had their promises and they were ready to go!

Those promises can literally save your life. Military history is full of stories confirming the power of Psalm 91. In this book we have collected a few of those stories, so you can do your own personal study of the psalm.

One particular story illustrates this remarkable protection most vividly. When a Pennsylvania lieutenant was accidentally discovered by the enemy while attempting to carry out a very important overseas mission, he immediately placed himself in the hands of God. All he could get out of his mouth was, "Lord, it's up to You now!" before the enemy shot him in the chest at point-blank range, knocking him flat on his back.

Thinking he was dead, his buddy grabbed the carbine out of his hands, paired it up with his own, and began blasting away with both guns. When his buddy finished, not one enemy was left.

Later, the lieutenant's sister in Pennsylvania got a letter relating this amazing story. The force of the bullet in the chest had only stunned her brother. Without thinking, he reached for the wound—but instead he felt his Bible in his pocket. Pulling it out he found an ugly hole in the cover. The Bible he carried had shielded his heart. The bullet had ripped through Genesis, Exodus, and kept going through book after book, stopping in the middle of the Ninety-first Psalm, pointing like a finger at verse seven—*"A thousand will fall at your side and ten thousand at your right hand; but it will not come near you."*

"I did not know such a verse was in the Bible, but precious God, I thank You for it," the lieutenant exclaimed. He did not realize this protection psalm even existed until the Lord supernaturally revealed it to him.

Perhaps your protection may not manifest itself as *dramatically* as it did with this army lieutenant, but your promise is just as reliable. This study is your chance to know that Psalm 91 can *literally save your life!* I encourage you to mark these Scriptures in your own Bible as we go straight through this psalm.

Now, let me add one more story so you'll understand why I'm so sure of that…

———

For much of my life, Sundays had been a comfort—but not this particular one! Our pastor looked unusually serious that day, as he announced that one of our most beloved and faithful deacons had been diagnosed with leukemia and had only a few weeks to live.

Only the Sunday before, this robust-looking man, in his mid-forties, had been in his regular place in the choir, looking as healthy and happy as ever. Now, one Sunday later, the entire congregation fell into a state of shock after hearing such an unexpected announcement. However, little did I know that this incident would pave the way to a message that would forever burn in my heart.

Surprisingly, I had gone home from church that day feeling very little fear, perhaps because I was numb from the shock of what I had heard. I vividly remember sitting down on the edge of the bed that afternoon and saying out loud, "Lord, is there any way to be protected from all the evils that are coming on the earth?"

I was not expecting an answer; I was merely voicing the thought that kept replaying over and over in my mind. I remember lying across the bed and falling immediately to sleep, only to wake up a short five minutes later. However, in those five minutes I had a very unusual dream.

In the dream I was in an open field, asking the same question that I had prayed earlier—"*Is there any way to be protected from all the things that are coming on the earth?*"

In my dream I heard these words: *"In your day of trouble call upon Me, and I will answer you!"*

Suddenly, I knew I had the answer. The ecstatic joy I felt was beyond anything I could ever describe. To my surprise, instantly there were hundreds with me in the dream out in that open field, joining me in praising and thanking God for the answer. It wasn't until the next day, however, when I heard the Ninety-first Psalm referred to on a tape by Shirley Boone, that

I suddenly knew in my heart that *whatever* was in that psalm was God's answer to my question. I nearly tore up my Bible in my haste to see what it said. And there it was in verse 15 —the *exact statement* God had spoken to me in my dream. I could hardly believe my eyes!

I believe that you who are reading this book are among the many Christians to whom God is supernaturally revealing this psalm. You were the ones pictured with me in my dream in that open field, who will, through the message in this book, get your answer to the question, "Can a Christian be protected through these turbulent times?"

Since the early 1970s, I have had many opportunities to share this message. I feel God has commissioned me to write this book to proclaim God's covenant of protection, *especially to the military*.

Once again…may you be sincerely blessed by it!

—**Peggy Joyce Ruth**

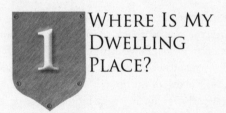

1 WHERE IS MY DWELLING PLACE?

He who dwells in the shelter of the Most High Will abide in the shadow of the Almighty. —Psalm 91:1

Have you ever been inside a cabin with a big roaring fire in the fireplace, enjoying a wonderful feeling of safety and security as you watch an enormous electrical storm pelting the landscape outside? It is a warm, wonderful sensation, knowing that you are sheltered and protected even as the storm rages.

That is what Psalm 91 is all about—shelter!

I am sure every one of you can think of something that represents *security* to you personally. When I think of security and protection I have a couple of childhood memories that automatically come to mind. My dad was a large, muscular man who played football during his high school and college years, but he interrupted his education to serve in the military during World War II.

While Dad was in the service, my mother and I—she was pregnant with my little brother—lived with my grandparents in San Saba, Texas. As young as I was I vividly remember one ecstatically happy day when my dad unexpectedly opened the door and walked into my grandmother's living room. Before that eventful day I had been tormented with fear, because some neighborhood children had told me that

I would never see my dad again. Like kids telling a ghost story, they taunted me that my dad would come home in a box. When he walked through that door, a sense of peace and security came over me and stayed with me for the rest of his time in the Army.

It was past time for my baby brother to be born, and I found out when I was older that Dad's outfit at the time was being relocated by train from Long Beach, California, to Virginia Beach, Virginia. When the train went through Fort Worth, Texas, on its way to Virginia, my dad got off and caught a ride from there to San Saba, hoping to see his new son. He then hitchhiked back until he caught up with the train shortly before it reached Virginia Beach.

The memory of his walking into that room still brings a feeling of peaceful calm to my soul. No doubt that incident set the stage for my years-long search, later on, for the security a heavenly Father's presence could bring.

Did you know that there is a place in God—a secret place—for those who want to seek refuge? It is a literal place of physical safety and security that God tells us about in this Psalm 91.

Dwelling in the shelter of the Most High is the Old Testament's way of teaching faith. This gives us the most intense illustration of the very essence of a personal relationship with God. Man has no innate built-in shelter. Alone, he stands unsheltered against the elements and must run to the Shelter Himself. In the first verse of Psalm 91, God offers us more than protection; it is as if He rolls out the hospitality mat and personally invites us in.

I cannot talk about this kind of peace and security without also having another vivid memory come to mind. My parents once took my younger siblings and me fishing on a lake near Brownwood, Texas, for an afternoon of fun.

Dad had a secluded place where we fished for perch. That was the second greatest highlight of the outing. I loved seeing the cork begin to bob, and then, suddenly, go completely out of sight. There were only a few things that could thrill me more than jerking back on that old cane pole and landing a huge perch, right in the boat. I think I was fully grown before I finally realized that Dad actually had an ulterior motive in taking us for an afternoon of perch fishing. He used the perch as bait for the trotline he had stretched out across one of the secret coves at the lake!

Dad would drive the boat over to the place where his line was located, cut off the boat motor, and inch the boat across the cove as he "ran the trotline." That's what he called it when he took the trotline into his hands and pulled the boat alongside all the strategically placed, baited hooks to see if any of them had caught a large catfish.

I said that catching the perch was the *second* greatest highlight of the outing. By far, the greatest thrill came when Dad would get to a place where the trotline would jerk almost out of his hand. Then we three siblings would watch, wide-eyed, as Dad wrestled with the line until finally, in victory, he would flip a huge catfish over the side of the boat, right onto the floorboards at our feet. Money couldn't buy that kind of excitement! Not even the circus and a carnival, all rolled into one, could compete with that kind of a thrill.

However, one of these outings turned out to be more eventful than most, quickly becoming an experience I will never forget. It had been beautiful when we started out, but by the time we finished fishing and headed toward the cove, everything had changed. A storm came upon the lake so suddenly there was no time to get back to the boat dock. The sky turned black, lightning flashed, and drops of rain fell with such force they actually stung when they hit. Moments later, we were being pelted by marble-size hailstones.

I saw the fear in my mother's eyes and I knew we were in danger. But before I had time to wonder what we were going to do, Dad had driven the boat to the rugged shoreline of the only island on the lake. Although boat docks surround the island now, back then it looked like an abandoned island with absolutely no place to take cover. Within moments Dad had us all out of the boat and ordered the three of us to lie down beside our mother on the ground. He quickly pulled a canvas tarp out of the bottom of the boat, knelt down on the ground beside us, and thrust the tarp up over all five of us.

That storm continued to rage outside the makeshift tent he had fashioned over us—the rain beat down, the lightning flashed, and the thunder rolled. Yet I could think of nothing else but how it felt to have my dad's arms around us. There was a certain calm under the protection of the shield my father had provided that is hard to explain now. In fact, I had never felt as safe and secure in my entire life. I remember thinking that I wished the storm would last forever. I didn't want anything to spoil the wonderful security I felt that day in *our secret hiding place*. I never wanted the moment to end.

Although I have never forgotten that experience, today it has taken on new meaning. Just as Dad put a tarp over us to shield us from the storm, our heavenly Father has a *secret place* in His arms that protects us from the storms that are raging in the world around us.

That secret place is literal but it is also conditional! In verse 1 of Psalm 91, God lists the condition we have to satisfy before He even mentions the promises included in His part. That's because our part has to come first. To abide in the shadow of the Almighty, *we must first choose to dwell in the shelter of the Most High.*

The question is, "How do we dwell in the shelter of the Most High?" It is more than an intellectual experience. This verse speaks of a dwelling place in which we can be physically protected if we run to Him. You may utterly believe that God is your refuge, you may give mental assent to it in your prayer time, you may teach Sunday school lessons on this concept of refuge, and you may even get a warm feeling every time you think of it. But unless you *do* something about it—unless you actually get up and *run to the shelter*—you will never experience it.

You might call that place of refuge a *love walk*. In fact, the secret place is, in reality, the intimacy and familiarity of the presence of God Himself. When our grandchildren—Cullen, 10, and Meritt, 7—stay the night with us, the moment they finish breakfast each runs to his own secret place to spend some time talking with God. Cullen finds a place behind the divan in the den, and Meritt heads behind the lamp table in the corner of our bedroom. Those places have become very special to them.

There are times when your secret place may have to exist in the midst of crisis circumstances with people all around you. A good example of that is a situation in which a U.S. Navy boy from Texas found himself. Running spiritually to his secret place is most likely what saved his ship from disaster.

He and his mother had both agreed to repeat Psalm 91 each day at a given time, to add agreement to his protection covenant. He later told of a time when his ship was under attack from the air and from an enemy submarine at the same time. All battle stations on the ship were in operation when the sub came within firing range and loosed a torpedo directly toward them. At that moment the young man realized it was the exact time that his mother would be saying Psalm 91, so he began quoting the psalm just as the torpedo wake appeared, heading directly toward their battleship. Then, when it was just a short distance away, it suddenly swerved, passing the stern and disappearing.

But, before the men had time to rejoice, a second torpedo was already coming straight toward them. "Again," he said, "as the second torpedo got almost to its target, it suddenly seemed to go crazy, turning sharply and passing by the bow of the ship. And with that, the submarine disappeared without firing another shot."

The whole ship must have been "under the shadow of the Almighty" because it didn't receive as much as a scratch from either the submarine or the planes flying overhead.

Where is your secret place? You, too, need the security and shelter of a secret place with the Most High.

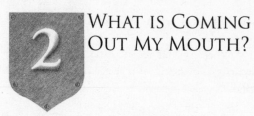

WHAT IS COMING OUT MY MOUTH?

I will say to the LORD, "My refuge and my fortress, my God, in whom I trust!" —Psalm 91:2

Notice that verse 2 above says, "I will say…" Circle the word *say* in your Bible, because we must learn to verbalize our trust. We answer back to God what He says to us in the first verse. There is power in saying His Word back to Him!

We are not told to simply *think* the Word. We are told to *say* the Word. For example, Joel 3:10 tells the weak to say, "I am a mighty man." Over and over we find great men of God, such as David, Joshua, Shadrach, Meshach, and Abednego, declaring their confessions of faith out loud in dangerous situations.

Notice what begins to happen on the inside when you say, *"Lord, You are my Refuge—You are my Fortress—You are my Lord and my God! I put my total trust in You!"*

The more we say it out loud, the more confident we become in His protection. Yet so many times, as Christians, we mentally agree that the Lord is our refuge—but that is not enough. Power is released when we say it out loud! When we say it and mean it, we are placing ourselves in His shelter. By voicing our acceptance and our reliance on His lordship and His protection, we open the door to the secret place.

One cannot miss the fact that this verse uses the word *my* three times: *my* refuge, *my* fortress, *my* God. The Psalmist makes a personal claim to God. The reason we can trust is that we know *who God is* to us. This verse makes the complete analogy: He is a *refuge* and a *fortress*. These metaphors are significant military terms. God Himself becomes the defensive site for us, protecting us from all invading enemies. He becomes—personally—our protection.

Have you ever tried to protect yourself from all the bad things that can happen? God knows we can't do it. Psalm 60:11 tells us that "…deliverance by man is in vain." God has to be our refuge before the promises in Psalm 91 will ever work.

We can go to the doctor once a month for a checkup. We can check our cars every day to make sure the motor, the tires, and the brakes are all in good working order. We can fireproof our houses and store up food for a time of need. We can take every additional precaution that the military offers, yet we still can't do enough to protect ourselves from every potential danger life has to offer. It's impossible.

At the same time, it isn't that any one of these precautions is wrong. It is that not one of these things, in and of itself, has the power to protect. God has to be the One to whom we run first. He is the only One who has an answer for whatever might come.

When I think of how utterly impossible it is to protect ourselves from all the evils in the world, I am reminded of sheep. A sheep has no real protection other than its shepherd. In fact, it is the only animal I can think of that has *no* built-in protection. It has no sharp teeth, no offensive odor to spray to drive off its enemies, no loud bark, and it certainly can't run fast enough to escape danger.

That's why the Bible calls us God's sheep! God is saying, "I want you to see Me as your source of protection. I am your Shepherd." He may use doctors, protective military/police equipment, bank accounts, and other things as well to meet our specific needs, but our hearts have to run to Him first as our Shepherd and our Protector. Then *He* will choose the method by which *He* desires to bring about our protection.

Some quote Psalm 91 as though it were some kind of *magic wand*, but there is nothing magical about this psalm. It is powerful and it works, but only because it is the Word of God, alive and active. And we confess it out loud simply because the Bible tells us to.

When I'm facing a challenge, I have learned to say, *"In this particular situation _____ [name the situation out loud], I choose to trust You, Lord."* The difference it makes when I proclaim my trust out loud is amazing.

Take notice of what flies out of your mouth in times of trouble. The worst thing that can happen is for something to come out that brings death. Cursing gives God nothing to work with. This psalm tells us to do just the opposite—speak life! Look at the examples in this next story, showing what these men did in a time of great trouble, during one of the most famous battles of modern history.

All of England stood amazed at what happened at Dunkirk in WWII, when the Nazis had thousands of British soldiers trapped at the edge of the water. They couldn't get the men off the beaches fast enough to get them back to safety in England. They were like sitting ducks when Nazi planes pelted those long stretches of white sand covered with soldiers, but the miraculous story that followed still stands out in history today.

One correspondent, C. B. Morelock, reported an unexplainable and miraculous occurrence: sixty German aircraft strafed more than four hundred men who were pinned down on the beach, without any place to take cover. And yet, although the men were repeatedly attacked by machine guns and bombed by enemy aircraft, not one single man was hit. Every man *in that group* left the beach without a scratch. Morelock stated, "I have personally been told by Navy men, who picked up those particular survivors from Dunkirk, that the men not only recited Psalm 91, but they shouted it aloud at the top of their lungs!" Saying our trust out loud releases faith.

Another time when God brought life to a death situation stands out in my mind. The whole family was rejoicing when our daughter-in-law, Sloan, received a positive pregnancy test report and found she was going to have the first grandchild on either side of the family. However, because she'd had a tubal pregnancy once before, which made her highly susceptible to having another, the doctor ordered a sonogram as a precautionary measure.

The disturbing result of the sonogram was "No fetus found, a great deal of water in the uterus, and spots of endometriosis." With only two hours' notice, emergency surgery was quickly underway, at which time the doctor performed a laparoscopy, drained the uterus, and scraped away the endometriosis. After the surgery the doctor's words were, "During the laparoscopy we carefully looked everywhere, and there was no sign of a baby, but I want to see you back in my office in one week to be sure fluid doesn't build back up."

When Sloan argued that the pregnancy test had been positive, he said there was a 99 percent chance the baby had naturally aborted and been absorbed into the uterine lining. Even so, after the doctor left the room, Sloan was the only one not fazed by his report. What she said next surprised everyone. She emphatically stated that even the doctor had left her with a 1 percent chance, and she was going to take it.

From that moment, no amount of discouragement from well-meaning friends—who didn't want her to be disappointed—had any effect on her. Never once did she veer away from confessing out loud Psalm 91, and another Scripture promise that she had found: "My child shall not die, but live, and tell of the works of the Lord" (Psalm 118:17). A treasured book that was very important to Sloan during this time was *Supernatural Childbirth* by Jackie Mize.

A strange look came on the technician's face the next week as she administered the ultrasound. She immediately called for the physician. Her reaction was a little disconcerting to Sloan until she heard the words, "Doctor, I think you need to come here quickly. I've just found a six-week-old fetus!"

It was nothing short of a miracle that such severe, invasive procedures had not damaged or destroyed this delicate life in its beginning stages. When I look at my grandson, it is hard to imagine life without him. I thank God for a daughter-in-law who believes in her covenant and is not ashamed to confess it out loud in the face of every negative report.

Our part of this protection covenant is expressed in verses 1 and 2 of Psalm 91. Note very carefully these words: "he who dwells" and "he who says." These words, which amount to *our responsibility* under the terms of this covenant, release God's power to fulfill His amazing promises.

These are given to us in verses 3 through 16, which we will look at in the next chapters.

3 Two Way Deliverance

For it is He who delivers you from the snare of the trapper and from the deadly pestilence. —Psalm 91:3

Have you ever seen a movie in which a fur trapper travels deep into the mountains in a cold climate? He baits big steel traps, covers them over with branches, and then waits for some unsuspecting animal to step into their jaws. Those traps are not there by chance. The trapper takes great care to place them in very strategic locations.

In times of war, a minefield is set up the same way. Those landmines are methodically placed in carefully selected locations.

These are pictures of what the enemy does to us. That is why he is called the *trapper!* The traps that are set for us are not there by accident. It is as if the trap has your name on it. They are custom made, placed, and baited specifically for each one of us. But like an animal caught in a trap, we then suffer through a slow, painful process. We don't die instantly. We are ensnared until the trapper comes to destroy us.

I will never forget a tragedy that happened to a good friend of mine, whose husband was stationed with the military overseas. Having quit in the middle of numerous career possibilities requiring a number of expensive moves, the young man finally joined the army without consulting anyone, including his wife. It was hard on this young wife who had faithfully undergone countless, abrupt alterations and changes of direction in her way of life. However, she was very supportive and constantly defended her husband's behavior.

Unfortunately, his low self-esteem and immature conduct made him a prime candidate to fall into one of the enemy's traps. He had been so accustomed to giving in to his flesh that when the enemy placed a beautiful, willing young girl in front of him, he temporarily forgot the faithful, young wife back home who had supported him through so much.

That was the straw that broke the camel's back. It is not repetitive to say, "Hurting people hurt people." This couple got caught in a downward spiral. Her years of pain and self-sacrifice left her hopeless, and the marriage was never able to be restored. Because the couple was ignorant of the schemes of the enemy, the trap that he so carefully laid accomplished exactly what *the trapper* set out to accomplish. The bait was set at the exact moment he was most vulnerable to fall.

The enemy knows exactly what will most likely hook us, and he knows exactly which thought to put into our minds to lure us into the trap. That is why Paul tells us in 2 Corinthians 2:11 that we are "not to be ignorant of the schemes [traps] of the enemy." In chapter 10 he says:

> For the weapons of our warfare are not of the flesh, but divinely powerful for the destruction of fortresses. We are destroying

speculations and every lofty thing
raised up against the knowledge
of God, and we are taking every
thought captive to the obedience of
Christ. (Vv. 4–5)

God not only delivers us from the snares laid by
the trapper (Satan), but according to the last part of
verse 3 He also delivers us from the deadly pestilence.
I always thought a pestilence was something that
attacked crops—bugs, locusts, grasshoppers, spider
mites, mildew, root rot. But after doing a word study
on the word *pestilence*, I found, to my surprise, that
pestilence attacks people—not crops!

Pestilence is "any virulent or fatal disease; an
epidemic that hits the masses of people."[2] These deadly
diseases attach themselves to a person's body with the
intent to destroy it. But God tells us in verse 3 that He
will deliver us.

There are all kinds of enemies: emotional
temptations, spiritual enemies, and physical enemies.
Doctors who study germs and bacterial attacks against
the body describe cellular battle scenes comparable
to military conflicts. Not surprisingly, each of these
enemies works in similar, strategic ways. Initially, I
was in a quandary after my word study, wondering if
God really meant literal pestilence. It took me a while
to see the spiritual side of enemy attacks, and the
internal workings of warfare in the body as a parallel
concept with disease.

Only man tries to choose between physical and
spiritual deliverance; the Scripture includes both
(notice how Jesus demonstrates that His power operates
at all levels with a very literal, physical fulfillment in

Matthew 8:16–17). When evil is served, it looks the same on the platter. Scripture deals with both through clear verses that promise physical healing and literal deliverance.

God is so good to confirm His Word when one seeks Him with an open heart. Right after I first began studying Psalm 91 and was trying to digest all of its protection promises, while also recognizing that God is the One who always sends good and not evil, Satan was on the other end trying to discourage my faith at every turn. Because I was very young in my walk with God, and was struggling hard to maintain it in the midst of a world that does not believe in the supernatural goodness of God, I was devastated when a thought came into my mind one morning as I was getting ready for church.

If God wants us to walk in health, why did He create germs? That one thought was attempting to completely dismantle my faith in the truth—that God had provided healing via the atonement.

In fact, I was so distraught I didn't even think I could motivate myself to go to church that morning. I remember going into my bedroom, where I literally fell on my face before God, asking Him how those two facts could possibly be reconciled. As clear as a bell, God spoke in my spirit: "Trust Me; get up and go and I will give you an answer."

I got up with mixed emotions. I had unmistakably heard God speak to my spirit, but I could see no way in which He could satisfactorily resolve that question that had stuck in my head. Why would God create a germ to make us sick, if He did, in fact, want us to walk in divine health?

I went to church that morning under a cloud

of heaviness, and I couldn't tell you what subject the pastor preached on. But somewhere in the middle of his sermon he made this statement: "God made everything good. Take germs, for instance—germs are nothing more than microscopic plants and animals that the enemy perverted and uses to spread disease." Then he stopped, and with a strange look on his face, said, "I have no idea where that thought came from. It was not in my notes."

He went right on with his sermon. I must admit I almost disturbed the entire service because I couldn't keep from bouncing up and down on the pew. The awesomeness of God was more than I could take in without its erupting out of me. God could not have done anything that would have strengthened my faith for healing more than that incident did that morning.

Do you sometimes feel you have opposition facing you from every side? Psalm 91:3 is addressing the enemy's assaults from both the physical and the spiritual domains.

One of our family members went to a certain country as a missionary and made the comment, "This is a country where there are lots of ways to die." Both the poor health conditions and the hostility in the country provided many dangers. As a soldier, you will encounter enemies that attack your mind (thoughts), some that attack your body internally (germs), and some who attack with weapons (people). This is your verse, ensuring your deliverance from all the varieties of harm.

Consider with me one more area of physical protection from harm. Often in war there are traps set that can toy with the human mind—tragedies in which innocent people are accidentally killed. I believe this is addressed in Scripture also. When Jesus sent the disciples out, He gave these instructions: "I send you out as sheep in the midst of wolves; so be shrewd as serpents and innocent as doves (Matthew 10:16)." It is an interesting piece of instruction to be told to have the cleverness of a snake (so as not to *be* harmed) but the innocence of a dove (so as not to *cause* harm).

Each year, at the Texas Rattlesnake Roundup, men often disassemble rattlesnakes with their knives for the gaping audience. They pry open the snake's mouth to reveal the fangs and milk it of its poison. Then with a knife they slice open the thick, scaly skin and reveal its extensive muscular structure. After seeing the internal workings, it becomes obvious that the snake is built for causing harm.

Not so with the dove. When a hunter cleans a dove, first he pulls off the feathers. There are no thick scales, no dangerous claws, no poisonous venom. The dove has nothing in him that causes harm.

In this analogy we are advised, as sheep among wolves, to be as clever as the snake but as innocent as the dove. This takes care of harm in two directions. I believe we are to claim the promise of this verse— for God to protect us from being harmed and from harming innocent people. Pray, for example, that God protects you from ever hitting a child on a bicycle, being involved in a wreck that kills another person, or causing someone to walk away from the faith.

Many a person has been traumatized from inadvertently hurting someone he never intended to hurt. In the military, a soldier's conscience can be easily wounded by causing unintended harm: accidental death or wounding via friendly fire; a medic's mistake on a patient; a plan that backfires; the death of a civilian by a stray bullet. Situations such as these can be traumatic, but God put this preventive promise in verse 3 for you to stand on for protection from both ways in which harm can destroy a life!

In the same way, notice the twofold aspect to this deliverance in verse 3: (1) from the snare of the trapper and (2) from the deadly pestilence. This covers being delivered from temptation and being delivered from harm. It is similar to the request in the Lord's Prayer: "Do not lead us into temptation, but deliver us from evil" (Matthew 6:13).

What good would it do to be delivered from harm only to be caught in a sin that destroys us? On the other hand, what good would it do to be delivered from a sin only to be destroyed by a deadly pestilence? This verse covers both.

Thank God for His deliverance from both traps and pestilence!

UNDER HIS WINGS!

He will cover you with His pinions, and under His wings you may seek refuge. —Psalm 91:4

When you picture a magnificent flying bird, it is usually not a chicken. I've never seen a chicken portrayed in flight—many eagles, but no chickens. We quote the Scripture from Isaiah 40:31 that talks about being borne up on the wings of eagles or with wings like eagles.

There is a difference, however, between being "on" His wings and being "under" His wings. This promise in Psalm 91 is not elaborating on the *flying* wing—but on the *sheltering* wing. One indicates *strength and accomplishment*, while the other denotes *protection and familiarity*. When you imagine the warmth of a nest and the security of being under the wings of the nurturing love of a mother hen with chicks, it paints a vivid picture of the sheltering wing of God's protection that the psalmist refers to in this passage.

Is everyone protected under the wings? Did you notice that it says He will cover you with His pinions (feathers), and under His wings you *may* seek refuge? Again, it's up to us to make that decision! We can seek refuge under His wings if we *choose* to.

The Lord gave me a vivid picture of what it means to seek refuge under His wings. My husband, Jack, and I live out in the country, and one spring our old mother hen hatched a brood of baby chickens. One afternoon, when they were scattered all over the yard, I suddenly saw the shadow of a hawk overhead. I then noticed something that taught me a lesson I will never forget. That mother hen did not run to those little chicks and jump on top of them to try to cover them with her wings. No!

Instead, she squatted down, spread out her wings and began to cluck. And those little chickens, from every direction, came running *to her* to get under those outstretched wings. Then the hen pulled her wings down tight, tucking every little chick safely under her. To get to those babies, the hawk would have to go through the mother.

When I think of those baby chicks running to their mother, I realize it is under His wings that we may seek refuge—*but we have to run to Him.*

> "He will cover you with His pinions,
> and under His wings, you may seek
> refuge."

That one little word *may* is a strong word! It is up to us. All that mother hen did was cluck and expand her wings to tell them where to come. This verse shows the maternal hovering side to His protection:

> Like flying birds so the LORD of
> hosts will protect Jerusalem. He
> will protect and deliver it; He will
> pass over and rescue it. Return

to Him from whom you have
deeply defected, O sons of Israel.
(Isaiah 31:5–6)

Jerusalem, Jerusalem…. How often
I wanted to gather your children
together, the way a hen gathers her
chicks under her wings, and you
were unwilling. (Matthew 23:37)

Notice the contrast between God's willingness
and our unwillingness—His "wanting" against our
"not willing"—His "would" against our "would not."
What an amazing analogy to show us that He offers
protection we don't accept.

It is interesting that Jesus uses the correlation of
maternal love to demonstrate His attachment to us.
There is a certain fierceness to motherly love that we
cannot overlook. God is deeply committed to us—yet
at the same time, *we can reject* His outstretched arms if
we so choose. It is available, but not automatic.

God does not run here and there, trying to cover
us. He said, "I have made protection possible. You run
to Me!" And when we do run to Him, in faith, the
enemy then has to go through God to get to us.

What a comforting thought!

A MIGHTY FORTRESS IS MY GOD

His faithfulness is a shield and bulwark. —Psalm 91:4

It is *God's* faithfulness to His promises that is our shield. It is not solely *our* faithfulness. God is faithful to the promises He has made.

When the enemy comes to whisper fearful or condemning thoughts in your mind, you can ward off his attack by saying, "My faith is strong because I know my God is faithful, and His faithfulness is my shield."

How often I've heard people say, "I can't dwell in the shelter of God. I mess up and fall short too many times. I feel guilty and unworthy."

Yet God knows all about our weaknesses. That is why He gave His Son. We can no more earn or deserve this protection than we can earn or deserve our salvation. The main thing is that, if we slip and fall, we must not stay down. Get up, repent, and get back under that shield of protection. Thankfully this verse says it is *His* faithfulness, not ours, that is our shield.

> If we are faithless, He remains faithful, for He cannot deny Himself. (2 Timothy 2:13)

My daughter once slipped and fell facedown in the busiest four-way intersection in our city. Embarrassment made her want to keep lying there so she didn't have to look up and show her face to so many people who would know her, for this was a small town. Yet the worst thing she could have done would have been to lie there!

This is a humorous illustration of what it looks like when we fall. When you think of my daughter lying facedown in that busy intersection, don't ever forget that the worst thing you can do after you fall spiritually is *fail to get up!*

This verse just expresses again God's commitment and faithfulness to being our shield of protection. It is His faithfulness that gets us back on our feet and moving again.

His unshakable faithfulness is a literal shield. I have an awesome mental picture of a huge shield out in front of me, completely hiding me from the enemy. The shield is God Himself. His faithfulness to His promises guarantees that He will remain steadfast, and His shield will be available to us forever. Whether we stay behind that protection is our choice. It was God's shield of protection Jake Weise experienced when a mortar exploded, killing and wounding those around him, yet leaving him without a scratch (see testimony page 216).

Psalm 91:4 also tells us that God's faithfulness is our *bulwark*. According to *Nelson's Bible Dictionary,* "a bulwark is a tower built along a city wall from which defenders shoot arrows and hurl large stones at the enemy."[3]

Think about that! God's faithfulness to His promises is not only a shield, but it is also a tower. From that tower God is faithful to point out the enemy so he can't sneak up on our blind side. *Webster's Dictionary* defines bulwark as "an earthwork or defensive wall, fortified rampart; a breakwater; the part of a ship's side above the deck." If you are onboard a ship, the word *bulwark* gives you a visual of His protection.

Throughout history there have been shields over individuals and groups who have stood on Psalm 91. Probably the most famous example comes from the First World War. On both sides of the Atlantic, religious publications reported the story of a "miracle regiment" that went through some of the most intense, bloodiest battles without a single combat casualty.[4]

The best sources say it was a British-American unit rather than exclusively an American one. Our researchers have enjoyed rebuilding this bridge between the event and its sources, and uncovering new leads to one of the most celebrated examples of the power of Psalm 91. Our sources say that every officer and enlisted man daily placed his trust in God by faithfully reciting the Ninety-first Psalm together, and that unit is known to have suffered not one single combat casualty. It is unthinkable to believe mere chance or coincidence could have prevented so many bullets and shells from finding their intended victims.

Dunkirk, in World War II, is another prime example. During that dreadful yet triumphant week in May of 1940, when the British army had been forced into total retreat and lay exposed on the sandy shores of Dunkirk, many miracles occurred. Lying hopeless and exposed, pinned down by Nazi planes and heavy artillery and armed only with their rifles, the brave troops were seemingly trapped with their backs to the channel, with no place to turn for protection. A British chaplain told of lying facedown in the sand for what seemed an eternity on the shell-torn beach at Dunkirk. Nazi bombers dropped their lethal charges, causing shrapnel to kick up sand all around him while other planes repeatedly strafed his position with their machine guns blazing.

Although dazed by the concussions around him, the British chaplain suddenly became aware that, in spite of the deafening roar of the shells and bombs falling all around him, he hadn't been hit. With bullets still raining down about him, he stood and stared with amazement at the outline of his own shape in the sand. It was the only smooth and undisturbed spot on the entire bullet-riddled beach. His heavenly shield must have fit the exact shape of his body.

On one of those same beaches at Dunkirk, C. B. Morelock, the famous war correspondent, was quoted as saying, "I lay with four hundred men who were machine-gunned systematically, up and down and bombed by sixty enemy aircraft, and in the end, there was not a single casualty."

Such a remarkable fortress was God at Dunkirk that Margaret Lee Runbeck, in her book *The Great Answer*, wrote:

> Dunkirk should be written about in Bible language. Someday, I have no doubt, it will be so written, for the race will look back on Dunkirk as it looks back on the Red Sea. That horde of tortured men who escaped will be remembered when people are in dire need, as the

children of Israel are remembered. Like the Red Sea, Dunkirk will be both adored and disbelieved. It will be explained away by scientific fact, as the skeptical have explained away all miracles in the sufficiently past tense. But it cannot be discredited yet, because too many people lived through it. Too many letters tell about it, and too many columns of words. But not one millionth of it has been told, nor ever will be. It happened quickly, rolling up like a nightmare, breaking over us in delirium. It was only after it receded, almost as quickly as it had come, that we began to understand it—no, for still we do not understand. But at least we saw what had happened. It began with prayer on the 26th of May; it ended with a Thanksgiving on the ninth of June.... No word had leaked out of the full extremity that was threatening three hundred and fifty thousand men stranded on the Continent. But people knew in their hearts this was rock bottom. And of course the men at the top were beside themselves. They knew human effort alone wasn't going to be enough. So the whole nation began to pray.... Then, gloriously, so great was the escape that even Winston Churchill called Dunkirk,

"The miracle of Deliverance."

Each of us faces times in our lives when we are trapped, when the odds are against us and when we look hopelessly defeated. Yet examples of God's protection in the form of a shield emerge in both modern and biblical accounts of combat. When men cry out to God, even skeptics recognize the shield and historians testify to the miracle.

Note that this verse in Psalm 91:4 declares God's faithfulness to us as both a shield and a bulwark in a double-layered analogy. The passage uses two military images of fortification and protection. God is our *tower*—our wall of protection in a collective sense; and He is our *shield*—a very personal and individualized defense. This verse indicates *double* protection.

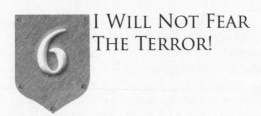

I WILL NOT FEAR THE TERROR!

You will not be afraid of the terror by night.

—Psalm 91:5

It is interesting to note that verses 5 and 6 of Psalm 91 cover an entire twenty-four-hour period, emphasizing day-and-night protection. But what is more important is that these two verses encompass every evil known to man.

The psalmist divides the list into four categories. We will look at those categories one at a time. The first—terror by night—includes all of the evils that come through man: kidnapping, robbery, rape, murder, terrorism, wars. These things also cause much dread—or horror—or alarm that comes from what man can do to you. Yet God says, "You will not be afraid of any of those things…because they will not approach you." The first thing verse 5 deals with is fear.

Over and over Jesus told us, "Do not fear!" Why do you think He continually reminds us not to be afraid? Because it is through faith in His Word that we are protected—and since fear is the opposite of faith, the Lord knows fear will keep us from operating in the faith that is necessary to receive. It is no wonder God addresses *the fear of terror* first.

So, how do we keep from being afraid? Very simply! In Psalm 91 God gives us instructions to quiet the fear that rises in our hearts. These words—"you will not be afraid of the terror by night and the arrows that fly by day"—also address the anxiety that comes the night before battle. Fear is never more prevalent than in wartime. Men have wrestled with such fear in many different ways. After a commanding officer confessed to his men that he experienced fear before every battle, one of his soldiers asked him, "How do you prepare for battle?" The officer took out his Bible, opened it, and showed him the Ninety-first Psalm.

Fear comes when we think we are responsible for bringing about this protection ourselves. Too often we think, *Oh, if I can just believe hard enough, maybe I'll be protected!* That's wrong thinking. The protection is already there. It has already been provided, whether we receive it or not. Faith is simply the choice to receive what Jesus has already done. The Bible gives classic examples of how to deal with terror.

The best answer is in the blood of Jesus. Exodus 12:23 tells us that when Israel put blood on the door facings, the destroyer could not come in. The animal blood they used then serves as a type and shadow, or a picture, of the blood of Jesus that ratifies our better protection—under our better covenant (Hebrews 8:6).

When we confess out loud, "I am protected by the blood of Jesus"—and believe it—the devil literally cannot come in. Remember, verse 2 tells us, "I will say to the Lord, my refuge and my fortress." It is heart and mouth—believing with our heart and confessing with our mouth.

Our physical weapons are operated with our hands, but we operate our *spiritual* weapons with our mouths. The blood is applied by *saying it* in faith. Confessing with our mouth and believing with our heart starts with the new birth experience and sets a precedent for receiving all of God's good gifts (Romans 10:9–10).

If we find ourselves afraid of the *terror by night,* that is our barometer letting us know we are not dwelling and abiding up close to the Lord in the shelter of the Most High, and believing His promises. Fear comes in when we are confessing things other than what God has said. When our eyes are not on God, fear will come. But let that fear be a reminder to repent.

> We walk by faith, not by sight.
> (2 Corinthians 5:7)

We have to choose to believe His Word more than we believe what we see—more than we believe the terror attack. Not that we deny the existence of the attack, for the attack may be very real. But God wants our faith in His Word to become more of a reality to us than what we see in the natural.

For example, the law of gravity is a fact! No one denies its existence, but just as the laws of aerodynamics can temporarily overcome the law of gravity, Satan's attacks can also be negated by a higher law—the law of faith and obedience to God's Word. Faith does not deny the *existence* of terror, but there are simply higher laws in the Bible for overcoming it.

David did not deny the existence of the giant. Fear has us compare the size of the giant to ourselves.

Faith, on the other hand, had David compare the size of the giant to the size of his God. David's eyes saw the giant, but his faith saw the promises (1 Samuel 17).

Can you imagine the terror you would feel having to make a crash landing, then learning that you are on an island occupied by Japanese soldiers in WWII? This next story is a perfect example of being delivered from *the terror by night.*

When one of our bombers, returning after a successful mission, ran out of gas, it was forced to land on the sandy beach of a Japanese-occupied island, several hundred miles from base.

"Chaplain, now is your chance to prove what you have been preaching," the men chided. "You have been telling us for months that we must pray and God will deliver us from the terror all around us. We need a miracle now." The chaplain began fervently praying and the first thing they noticed was that their landing had gone unnoticed by the enemy. Night fell and he continued to pray.

About 2 a.m. they hear a new sound on the beach side, and in spite of the terror that almost overwhelmed the group they crept into the water's edge so silently that they didn't even disturb the chaplain, who was still kneeling in prayer.

They were able to make out the dim outline of a large barge, but no voices or footsteps could be heard. If the crew was asleep, there was no sentry on the deserted deck. Aboard the barge, the deck was covered with oil drums filled with high-octane gasoline. They could hardly restrain a shout of joy. It seemed like a dream. This drifting barge had brought them the one thing in all the world that could get their bomber off the island and back to the home base. They ran back across the sand and embraced their startled chaplain, used their in-flight refueling hose, and took off thunderously down the beach runway.

A later investigation revealed that the skipper of a U.S. tanker, after finding himself in submarine infested waters, had ordered his gasoline cargo removed to lessen the danger from a torpedo hit. Barrels of gasoline were placed on barges and set adrift—some six hundred miles from where their plane had landed. In just a few weeks that oil barge had aimlessly drifted the whole six hundred miles across the Pacific, then beached itself just fifty steps from the stranded men.

And all within twelve hours of their crash. The chaplain's prayers had been heard and they were delivered from the terror by night.

We do not have to be afraid of the terror of what man can do to harm us. Praise God for our higher law! God's laws triumph over man's laws.

I WILL NOT FEAR
THE ARROW

You will not be afraid of...the arrow that flies by day.

—Psalm 91:5

The second category of evil is the arrow that flies by day. An arrow is something that pierces or wounds spiritually, physically, mentally, or emotionally. Arrows are intentional. This category indicates you are in a *spiritual* battle zone; specific enemy assignments are directed toward your life to defeat you.

Arrows are deliberately sent by the enemy and are carefully aimed at the spot that will cause the most damage. They are targeted toward the area where our mind is not renewed by the Word of God—perhaps an area where we are still losing our temper, or where we are still easily offended, or perhaps an area of rebellion or fear.

Seldom does the enemy attack us in an area where we are built up and strong. He attacks us where we struggle. That's why we have to run to God! And when we do battle using our spiritual weapons, the enemy's arrows will not approach us.

God tells us in Ephesians 6:16 that we have a "shield of faith" to extinguish all the flaming darts of the enemy. This covers the area of intentional danger. Someone bends the bow and pulls back the bowstring. The arrows are aimed and released. These are not regular, everyday arrows; they are on fire. Yet God doesn't say that most of them will miss us. He says we can extinguish "all" of them. When arrows are sent to wound us spiritually, physically, mentally, emotionally, or financially, God wants us to ask and believe by faith that He will pick us up and deliver us from calamity.

Our daughter had a friend, Julee, living in an apartment in Fort Worth, Texas. She was getting ready for church one Sunday morning when someone knocked on her door. Never dreaming it wasn't someone she knew, she opened the door, only to be almost knocked over by a strange man who shoved his way in and attacked her.

Remembering what God said, "You will not be afraid of the arrow…it will not approach you," Julee started using the Scripture as her defense. In the natural there was no way for a young girl to escape from a strong man, but her confidence in her God enabled her not to give up!

It took forty-five minutes of spiritual battling as he came at her time after time. But her persistence in quoting the Word brought confusion and immobility on him, thwarting every attempted attack. Finally, during one of those times when he was at a standstill, she was able to get out the door and escape unharmed.

Later, after he was apprehended and held in custody, she found that he had sexually assaulted numerous young women, and she was the only one of his victims who had been able to escape without harm.

We have a covenant with God, telling us not to be afraid of the arrow that flies by day. Assignments will rise up, but don't be afraid of the arrows. He has promised that they will not hit their target.

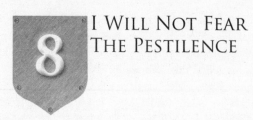

I WILL NOT FEAR THE PESTILENCE

You will not be afraid of...the pestilence that stalks in darkness. —Psalm 91:5–6

Fear gripped my heart, and beads of perspiration popped out on my forehead as I feverishly ran my fingers over what felt like a lump in my body. How I dreaded the monthly self-examination that the doctor had suggested. My fingertips were as cold as ice from the panic I had worked up, just thinking about what I might find and dreading the turn my life might take from there.

On that particular day it turned out to be a false alarm, but the dread of what I might find in the coming months was constantly in the back of my mind, until the promise of Psalm 91:6 came alive in my heart. If you fight fears of fatal diseases, then this is the Scripture for you to take hold of.

The third category of evil God names is *pestilence*. This is the only evil He names twice! Since God doesn't waste words, He must have a specific reason for repeating this promise.

Have you noticed that when a person says something more than once, it is usually because he wants to emphasize a point? God knew the pestilence and the fear that would be running rampant in these end days. The world is almost overrun with fatal epidemics, hitting people by the thousands, so God catches our attention by repeating this promise.

It's as though God is saying, "I said in verse 3, 'You are delivered from the deadly pestilence,' but did you really hear Me? Just to be sure, I am saying it again in verse 6: 'You do not have to be afraid of the deadly pestilence!'"

This is so contrary to what the world teaches us that we have to renew our thinking. Only then can we understand that we do not have to be afraid of the sicknesses and diseases endemic to the world today.

When I first started studying this psalm, I remember thinking, *I don't know whether I have the faith to believe these promises!* This thought stretched my faith and my mind until I thought it would snap like a rubber band.

But God then reminded me that faith is not a feeling. Faith is simply *choosing* to believe what He says in His Word. The more I chose to believe God's Word, the more I *knew* that I could trust and rely on it completely.

Our inheritance is not limited to what is handed down to us genetically. Our inheritance can be what Jesus provided for us if we believe the Word and put it to work.

> Christ redeemed us from the curse
> of the Law, having become a curse
> for us. (Galatians 3:13)

The pestilence mentioned here in Psalm 91 is spelled out in detail in Deuteronomy 28. The above verse from Galatians then tells us that we are *redeemed* from every curse (including pestilence) if we will *believe* and *appropriate* the promise.

Never before in our history has there been so much talk of terrorism and germ warfare, but to the surprise of so many people, God is not shocked or caught off guard by these things. Do we think chemical warfare is bigger than God? Long before man discovered biological weapons, God made provision for the protection of His people—if they would believe His Word.

> These signs will accompany those who have believed...if they drink any deadly poison, it will not hurt them. (Mark 16:17–18)

According to *Strong's Concordance,* the word *drink* in this Scripture comes from a Greek word that means "to drink, to absorb, to inhale or to take into the mind." No evil has been conceived by man against which God has not provided a promise of protection, for any of His children who will choose to believe it and act on it.

What about the fear that has come on mankind regarding our polluted water supplies and the contamination of our foods by pesticides? I believe that the Word of God advocates using wisdom, but all the precautions in the world cannot protect us from every harmful thing that could be in our food and water.

I am sure you have all found yourselves in conditions (even in survival training) where the food and water were questionable. Therefore, God's instruction to bless our food and water before eating is not simply some ritual to make us look more spiritual. Rather, it is another provision for our safety, playing an important role in God's protective plan.

It is God's goodness that made these provisions before we ever asked! This is not for everyone; it is for those who *believe and know the truth*. In biblical days, when they mentioned pestilence they were thinking of diseases such as leprosy. Luke 21:11 tells us that one of the signs of the end times will be an outbreak of pestilence. And today we have many widespread diseases such as AIDS, cancer, malaria, heart disease, tuberculosis. Yet no matter what pestilence we might be facing, His promise never ceases to be true.

The enemy may try to cause sudden surprises to catch us unaware and knock us down, but God is faithful. His Word is true no matter what the circumstances look like at times.

For example, I have never seen anyone stand as steadfast as Rene Hood did when the doctor diagnosed her with the last stages of lupus. Some of her major organs were shutting down and the doctors had given up. But she refused to turn loose of God's covenant promise of health and she is alive and well today, against all odds, preaching the Word of God in prisons all over the nation (see her testimony on page 200).

I shudder to think what we might open ourselves up to without the promise of Psalm 91, and without the determination to stand firm and refuse to entertain fearful thoughts. What we allow our mind to dwell on is *our* choice. Therefore, if we desire to operate in this protection covenant, taking authority over negative thoughts and emotions is imperative. It is amazing how the simple phrase "I am just not going there" will dispel those fear thoughts immediately.

I'm sure this promise of protection from plagues and pestilence reminded the Jews of Israel's complete immunity from the Egyptian plagues in the land of Goshen. The destroyer could not come in where the blood was applied.

Even in this Old Testament psalm God has declared, "You will not be afraid of the pestilence that stalks in darkness—it will not approach you."

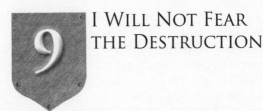

I WILL NOT FEAR
THE DESTRUCTION

You will not be afraid of…the destruction that lays waste at noon. —Psalm 91:5–6

This fourth category of evil is *destruction*. Destruction takes in the evils over which mankind has no control—those things the world ignorantly calls acts of God: tornadoes, floods, hail, hurricanes, and fire. Yet God very plainly tells us we are not to fear destruction. These natural disasters are not from Him.

In Mark 4:39, Jesus rebuked the storm and it became perfectly calm. This demonstrates that God is not the author of such things, for Jesus never would have contradicted His Father by rebuking something sent by Him.

There is no place in the world you can go and be safe from every destruction—every natural disaster. We can never anticipate what might come when we least expect it. But no matter where you are in the world, God says to run to His shelter where you will not be afraid of the destruction…it will not approach you!

Our granddaughter, Jolena, and her husband, Heath Adams, U.S. Air Force, were stationed in Turkey just before the war was declared in Iraq. Soon after her arrival in Turkey, Jolena started working as a lifeguard at a pool. One day, at the end of June she began to hear a loud noise that sounded much like a plane breaking the sound barrier; then everything started to shake. Everyone around her began to panic when the water splashed in the pool from an earthquake she later found to be a 6.3 on the Richter scale. Swimmers were desperately trying to get out of the water to find some place of safety, while children clung to Jolena and screamed in fear.

Everywhere people were hollering, but Jolena said she felt a peace and a calm come over her. She started praying in a loud voice, pleading the blood of Jesus over the Air Force base and over the people there. Suddenly, everyone around her became perfectly quiet and began listening to her pray. No one on the base was seriously hurt, but just five minutes from there, apartment buildings collapsed and more than a thousand people were killed in the quake. Heath was at work as he watched the wall of a building completely crumble and fall to the street.

Every day Jolena and Heath had been praying Psalm 91 protection over their home, and it certainly paid off. The base suffered a great deal of structural damage; the PX and the gym were completely lost; and many of the houses were destroyed. Furniture, TVs, and stereos were ruined as well, causing literally thousands of dollars' worth of damage. Many of the houses had such huge cracks from the earthquake you could actually see through the walls. On a home just one block from their home the staircase had completely separated from the wall.

Their miracle was that, other than one tiny crack over one of the doorways, there was not one bit of damage to their house or to any of their furnishings. While many of their friends had to move out of their homes so they could be repaired, Jolena and Heath didn't have to go through any of that. God wants us to take seriously His Promise that *we do not have to fear destruction, it will not approach us.*

I have to share one other protection-from-destruction miracle because these dangers can approach fast and in broad daylight; therefore, you must know your covenant promises. Jack and our son, Bill—not knowing there was an old underground gas well at the back of our three-hundred-acre property— were burning brush. As you can imagine, when the fire reached the gas well it literally exploded, sending fire in every direction and igniting a nearby grass field. Immediately the fire was completely out of control. With no water lines back there at the time, they were fighting to no avail. The barrel of water they had in the back of the pickup didn't even make a dent in the flames.

Seeing that the fire was getting dangerously close to other fields that led directly to the surrounding homes, Jack flew up to the house to call the fire department, sent me to meet them at the crossroads so they wouldn't get lost, and dashed back, only to find that the fire was out. Bill, looking as though he had been working in the coal mines, was sitting on a tree stump trying to catch his breath.

Jack said, "How on earth were you able to put out the fire—there was no way!" Bill's next words—"I called on God"—said it all. You, too, can be delivered from destruction at noon. For those out-of-control days, God is always there.

Every evil known to man will fall into one of these four categories we have named in verses 5 through 6: terror, arrows, pestilence, or destruction. And the amazing thing is that God has offered us deliverance from them all.

God has said in His Word we will not be afraid of terror, arrows, pestilence, or destruction. These things will not approach us if we dwell in His shelter and abide in His shadow. This psalm is not filled with exceptions or vague conditions as if trying to give God an out—an excuse to fail to fulfill the promises. Rather, it is a bold statement of what He wants to do for us.

We can receive anything God has already provided. The secret is knowing that *everything for which God has made provision* is clearly spelled out and defined in the Word of God. If you can find where God has offered it, you can have it! It is never a case of God holding back. His provision is already there—waiting to be received.

God is faithful to all the promises He has made. He didn't create man and then leave man to himself. When He created us He automatically made Himself responsible to care for us and meet our every need. And when He makes a promise, He is faithful to what He has promised. This psalm seems to build from one promise to the next. Men are judged by their faithfulness to their own word. Real men are only as good as their word. God is more faithful than even the most truthful man, for He has the power to carry out His Word.

Don Beason (see testimony, page 144), a WWII veteran whom I have had the pleasure of knowing, gave me this documentation on the tornadoes which devastated Grand Island, Nebraska, on June 3, 1980.

Three, possibly four tornadoes grouped together and slashed their way down Bismark Road and South Locust Street. Roger Wakimoto, an assistant to Dr. Fujital of Chicago University, said his preliminary research shows the movement of the tornadoes during the June 3 storm was extremely erratic. According to Wakimoto these were very unusual tornadoes, seeming to have changed directions more than once. Fujital also said that the smaller tornadoes began spinning around the larger one, and as they began picking up debris they locked together and formed one large tornado. Don Davis, chief meteorologist with the National Weather Service in Grand Rapids said there was a counterclockwise movement of the front, the main tornado came in the second movement, and the smaller tornadoes followed behind, creating one of the worst of its kind ever recorded. In all, there were at least seven tornadoes all going in different directions, but four of them came together to make a large one that did most of the damage.

The tornado at Grand Island was headed directly for Mr. Beason's office, and the first of two erratic, inexplicable turns it made occurred only a few yards before it reached him. It ruined the office directly across the street, but not even a window was cracked in his own.

The second of the two radical changes of direction came just before it would have swept through Mr. Beason's farm. The farms next to his were all destroyed. The city map showing the tornado's path confirmed that it went straight for his office, then turned in front of his doorstep and then went straight for his farm, turning once again just short of his property line.

The chart dramatically showed that the two major, utterly surprising changes of direction were directly connected to his real estate. There was no explanation in the natural for the two sudden turns of the tornado—but no one could convince Mr. Beason it was not the direct result of God's Psalm 91 protection he had been claiming—"I will not be afraid of the destruction [natural disasters] that lay waste at noon."

A few years later the TV station reported a mile-wide tornado heading once again toward Grand Island. Mr. Beason said, "I went outside and rebuked it and commanded it to turn away and disappear. A minute or two later when I went back into the house, the TV announcer said the tornado had lifted out of sight. More Psalm 91 protection!"

Faith is not a tool to manipulate God into giving you something you want. Faith is simply the means by which we accept what God has already made available. Our goal needs to be the renewal of our minds, to such an extent that we have more faith in God's Word than in what we can perceive with our physical senses. God does not make promises that are out of our reach.

When the Lord first began showing me these promises and my mind was struggling with "How can this be?" doubts, He took me to a portion of His Word that helped set me free:

> What then? If some did not believe, their unbelief will not nullify the faithfulness of God, will it? May it never be! Rather, let God be found true, though every man be found a liar, as it is written, "THAT YOU MAY BE JUSTIFIED IN YOUR WORDS, AND PREVAIL WHEN YOU ARE JUDGED." (Romans 3:3–4)

God is telling us, even though there may be some who *don't* believe, that their unbelief will never nullify His promises to the ones who *do* believe. Paul, in Romans, quoting from the Old Testament, gives us an important reminder that what we as individuals choose to believe and confess will cause us to prevail during times of judgment.

Without the promises of protection throughout the Word of God, and especially without our Psalm 91 covenant—listing all forms of protection made available in one psalm—we might feel rather presumptuous if, on our own, we *asked* God to protect us from all the things listed in these last four verses (see chapters 6 through 9).

In fact, we probably would not have the nerve to ask Him for all of this coverage. But He *offered* this protection to us before we even had a chance to *ask*!

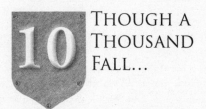

10 THOUGH A THOUSAND FALL...

A thousand may fall at your side and ten thousand at your right hand, but it shall not approach you.... For you have made the LORD, my refuge, even the Most High, your dwelling place. —Psalm 91:7, 9

Do we ever stop to consider what God is saying to us in verse 7? Do we have the courage to trust God's Word enough to believe He means this literally? Is it possible for this to be true, and for us to miss out on these promises?

Jesus answers the last question in Luke 4:27: "There were many lepers in Israel in the time of Elisha the prophet; and none of them was cleansed." Only Naaman the Syrian was healed when he obeyed in faith.

Not everyone will receive the benefits of this promise in Psalm 91. Only those who believe God and hold fast to His promises will profit; nonetheless, it is available. And to the measure that we trust Him, we will in the same measure reap the benefits of that trust.

What an awesome statement! God wants us to know that even though there will be a thousand falling by our side and ten thousand at our right hand, it does not negate the promise that destruction will not approach the one who chooses to believe and trust His

Word. *The Amplified Bible* says, "It shall not approach you *for any purpose*" (emphasis added). He means exactly what He says.

It is no accident that this little statement is tucked away right here in the middle of the psalm. Have you noticed how easy it is to become fearful when disaster strikes all around you? We begin to feel like Peter must have felt as he walked on the water to Jesus. It is easy to see how he started sinking into the waves when he saw all the turbulence of the storm raging around him.

God knew there would be times when we would hear so many negative reports, see so many needs, and encounter so much danger around us we would feel overwhelmed. That is why He warned us ahead of time that thousands would be falling all around us. He did not want us to be caught off guard.

But at that point we have a choice to make. The ball is then in our court! We can either choose to run to His shelter in faith and the storm will not approach us, or we can passively live our lives the way the world does, not realizing there is something we can do about it.

Psalm 91 is the *preventive* measure that God has given to His children, against every evil known to mankind. No place else in the Word are all of the protection promises (including help from angels, as well as promises ensuring our authority) accumulated in one covenant to offer such a total package for living in this world. It is both an *offensive* and *defensive* measure, for warding off every evil before it has had time to strike. This is not only a cure, but a plan for *complete prevention*!

What tremendous insight, after our minds have been renewed by the Word of God, to realize, contrary

66

to the world's thinking, that we do not have to be among the ten thousand who fall at our right hand.

> You will only look on with your
> eyes and see the recompense of the
> wicked. (Psalm 91:8)

You will see recompense (payment) being doled out at times. There is judgment. Every sin will be exposed sooner or later, and paid for. An evil dictator falls, an unrighteous aggressor is stopped, a tyrant faces his crimes against humanity, a wrong is rectified—the recompense of the wicked speaks of justice. Wars have been fought where one side had a righteous cause, and consequently, good won over evil. The justness of God is that evil will not triumph—that Hitlers do not win, that communistic governments fall, that darkness does not extinguish light.

Verse 8 says that we will "only look on and see" it happening. The word *only* tells us that we will be protected by not *experiencing* the evil, even though we will see it. And, it denotes detachment in that the evil we see will not get inside of us. We are set apart in that we will not allow our enemy's hate to change us.

Let's look for just a moment at this Scripture with our faith in mind—do we sometimes fall into unbelief? Faith in God, in His Son, Jesus Christ, and in His Word is counted in God's eyes as righteousness. But when we are in unbelief, to some degree we are placing ourselves in the category of the wicked. Sometimes, even as a Christian, I have been an unbelieving believer when it comes to receiving all of God's Word.

Jesus says in Matthew 5:18, "Not the smallest letter or stroke shall pass from the Law until it is all accomplished." Even if believers have never utilized this psalm in its full potential, the truth has never passed away or lost one ounce of its power.

Late one night, soon after building our new home in the country, our family was faced with a severe weather alert. The local radio station warned that a tornado had been sighted just south of the country club—the exact location of our property. We could see several of the React Club vehicles parked on the road below our hill, as the members watched the funnel cloud that seemed to be headed straight for our house.

I had never seen such a strange, eerie color in the night sky, or experienced such a deafening silence in the atmosphere. You could actually feel the hair on your body stand on end. Some of our son's friends were visiting, and to their surprise, Jack quickly ordered our family to get outside with our Bibles (even though we were in our pajamas) and start circling the house—quoting Psalm 91 and taking authority over the storm. Jack had our children out speaking directly to the storm, just like Jesus did.

The eerie silence suddenly turned into a roar, with torrents of rain coming down in what seemed like bucketsful. Finally, Jack had a peace that the danger had passed, even though by sight nothing had changed.

We walked back into the house just in time to hear the on-location reporter call the radio announcer and exclaim over the air, with so much excitement he was almost shouting, "This is nothing short of a miracle—the funnel cloud south of the Brownwood Country Club has suddenly lifted up and vanished into the clouds."

You should have seen those kids jumping and hollering! It was the first time my son's friends had observed the supernatural at work. However, their surprise was no greater than that of my daughter's college professor the next day. He asked the students in his class what they were doing during the storm. Several said they were in the bathtub under a mattress. Some were in closets, and one was in a storm cellar.

You can imagine the astonishment when he got around to our daughter, Angelia, who said, "With the tornado headed our direction, my family was circling the house, quoting from Psalm 91: 'We *will not be afraid...of the destruction that lays waste...it will not approach us.'*"

Many people think of the gospel as an insurance policy, securing only their eternity and their comfort after disaster strikes. They are depriving themselves of so much. Perhaps we all need to ask ourselves the question, "What kind of coverage do I have—fire or life?" God's Word is more than merely an escape from hell; it is a handbook for living a victorious life in this world.

Jesus lived in a realm in which He literally was not approached by evil. There is a difference between the destruction of the enemy and persecution for the gospel's sake. As Paul writes in 2 Timothy 3:12, "Indeed, all who desire to live godly in Christ Jesus will be persecuted."

There are times when we will be mistreated because of our stand for the cause of Christ. Psalm 91 is a very distinct concept dealing with natural disasters, accidents, sickness, and destruction. Jesus suffered persecution but He did not face calamity, disaster, and mishap. Accidents never even approached Him.

This distinction is easy to understand if you separate persecution from freak accidents and mishaps.

There is a place where calamity literally does not even approach us. This would be seemingly impossible to imagine—especially in combat situations. Yet, to look at this verse in its true context, with its thousands falling on either side, we observe the strongest description of casualty and calamity named in the psalm. If this verse isn't a description of actual combat, I don't know what is. Yet tied to it is a promise of protection beyond anything that could otherwise be envisioned. This portrayal of people falling is directly connected to the promise that it will not even come near us. Two opposite poles joined together!

Is this possible? In Leslie Gerald King's testimony (see page 235), a group of prayer warriors back in his hometown were in agreement on the power of God in this psalm, and it gave the soldiers in his company this supernatural type of *not-being-approached* protection in a volatile setting where men were falling on every side. King said the protection was so real that for one year he could almost reach out and touch it, but the soldiers knew the day when prayer let up and called home to ask what had happened.

There was a sudden shift when the people backed off from praying, took the prayer board down at the church, and got occupied with other things—the soldiers in his company immediately experienced the battle approaching at a personal level. The psalm is making its strongest offer of protection right in the very midst of chaos. And it is a type of protection that stands in a category all its own.

Too many people see Psalm 91 as a beautiful promise that they file right alongside all of their other quality reading material. It makes them feel comforted every time they read it. But I do not want anyone to read this book and fail to see the *superior significance* of these promises in this psalm. These are not written for our inspiration, but for our protection. These are not words of comfort *in* affliction, but words of deliverance *from* affliction.

No Plague Comes Near My Family!

No evil will befall you, nor will any plague or calamity come near your tent. —Psalm 91:10

Are you worried about your family at home? This part of Psalm 91 is written in capital letters just for you. After God repeats our part of the condition in verse 9, He then reemphasizes the promise in verse 10: "Nor will any plague come near your tent." At this point in the psalm the Bible makes this covenant more comprehensive than merely being about ourselves.

God has just added a new dimension to the promise: the opportunity to exercise faith, not only for ourselves but also for the protection of our entire household. If these promises were only available to us as individuals, they would not be completely comforting. But because God has created within us both an instinct to be protected and a need to protect those who belong to us, He has assured us here that these promises are for each of us and our households.

It appears that the Old Testament leaders had a better understanding of this concept than we do. That is why Joshua chose for himself *and for his household.*

> If it is disagreeable in your sight to
> serve the Lord, choose for yourselves
> today whom you will serve: whether

> the gods which your fathers served
> which were beyond the River, or
> the gods of the Amorites in whose
> land you are living; but as for me
> and my house, we will serve the
> LORD. (Joshua 24:15)

As Joshua made the decision that his household would serve God with him, he was influencing their destiny and declaring their protection at the same time. In much the same way, Rahab bargained with the Israeli spies for her whole family (Joshua 2:13).

When our hearts are truly steadfast and we are trusting in His faithfulness to fulfill His promises, we will not be constantly afraid something bad will happen to one of our family members.

> He will not fear evil tidings; his
> heart is steadfast, trusting in the
> LORD. (Psalm 112:7)

Negative expectations will begin to pass away and we will start expecting good reports. According to this verse, we can grab our ears and proclaim, "These ears were made to hear good tidings!" The fear of bad tidings can make our very existence miserable. The fear of the phone ringing in the night, of that knock on the door, of the siren of an ambulance, of that letter of condolence. For all those possible moments, this is the verse that promises that a steadfast heart will not live in constant fear of tragic news.

Someone once said, "Fear knocked, faith answered, and no one was there."[5] When fear knocks, let your mouth say out loud, "I will not fear evil tidings; my heart is steady, trusting in You!"

We exercise a certain amount of authority for those "under our roof." Our family has had several notable experiences of God delivering people from calamity who were "on our land, in our home, or near our dwelling." Buddy protection has had a very long tradition in the military, but this story of my grandson stands in a class all its own.

Staff Sergeant Heath Adams had gone hunting with one of his Air Force buddies. Seeing a coyote, the friend traded places with Heath and jumped in the passenger seat of the pickup for a better view. Since the bipod on his rifle was longer than the gun barrel, he couldn't put the barrel down so he rested the .30-06 rifle between his legs, facing up. Somehow the jostling of the pickup caused the gun to fire, sending a 180 grain bullet through his chest and arm pit. The friend started screaming, and to Heath's dismay, all he saw was a bloody mass of muscle and tissue. The concussion from the blast alone was so strong it blew out the back window.

In an instant Heath pulled off his jacket, put it under his friend's arm, and then applied pressure to the arm and chest in an effort to stop the bleeding. Simultaneously he was holding pressure against the arm, gripping the steering wheel to hold it steady as he drove rapidly on the icy road, and searching for service with his cell phone—all without mishap, which was nothing short of a miracle.

Heath was able to get through with his cell phone to the 911 dispatcher, but he still had to drive the twenty-two-mile stretch to the nearest town. That, too, may have been part of God's plan because it gave him time to declare God's promise from Psalm 91. Heath said later that he was not about to let his friend die because he was not born again and he was determined no flaming arrow of the enemy was going to take his buddy out before he made Jesus the Lord of his life. The whole ordeal was miraculous as he underwent six hours of surgery and came out with no permanent damage.

God was certainly at work that day. Normally it would have been disastrous to drive fifty or sixty miles per hour on an icy Montana road in December—especially while steering left-handed during a life-and-death situation. But Heath said no matter how fast he drove, God gave the pickup enough traction that never once was there even a hint of the wheels sliding.

Later they went back to the same place, and try as they might they could not get cell phone service anywhere in that twenty-two-mile stretch. Of course, the biggest miracle of all was that a .30-06 bullet through the chest and arm neither hit a vital organ nor damaged the arm beyond repair. Heath's friend was blessed beyond words to have been with someone who knew and loved God, and held fast to God's Word.

In Matthew 13:32, Jesus makes reference to the mustard seed starting as an herb but growing into a tree with the birds nesting in the branches. Others can find protection in our faith as well, when we plant the seed of the Word.

Towns are big collections of families, and family protection could not have been more clearly demonstrated than by what took place in Seadrift, Texas, in World War II. The town's citizens decided to pray Psalm 91 collectively over every one of their husbands, sons, grandsons, cousins, uncles, and friends who were going to war. A bulletin board was made with photos of every serviceman and a commitment made that every single day intercessors would cover them in prayer. Every time they met they would read from Psalm 91.

It seemed that everyone had a family member who had gone to fight. What a testimony to this promise of family protection when every single man returned home from war from all over the world. This town did not suffer a single combat casualty, while so many other towns and families experienced much grief and heartache, and often, multiple casualties. This is one of the many reasons why this psalm is known as "the soldier's prayer" (see testimony on page 138).

The same is true for you. The beauty of this psalm is that when someone prays for more than himself, he brings the entire family under the shield of God's Word. It introduces an added dimension to us as individuals to be able to apply the richness of this covenant to our entire household. Many support groups of wives, mothers, and sisters have evolved to pray for the soldiers in the field. What a joy to know you have promises in Psalm 91 that will not only protect you, but also those in your family and near your dwelling.

12 ANGELS WATCHING OVER ME

For He will give His angels charge concerning you, to guard you in all your ways. They will bear you up in their hands, that you do not strike your foot against a stone.

—Psalm 91:11–12

In verses 11 and 12, God makes another unique promise concerning an additional dimension of our protection. This is one of the most precious promises of all, and He put it right here in Psalm 91. In fact, this is one of the promises Satan used to test Jesus.

Most Christians read past this promise with very little thought about the magnitude of what is being said. Only after we get to heaven will we realize all the things from which we were spared because of the intervention of God's angels on our behalf.

I am sure you have read stories about missionaries whose lives were spared because would-be murderers saw large bodyguards protecting them when, in fact, there was no one there in the natural. The same is true with soldiers who have had similar experiences in combat. We have to wonder what the Iraqi soldier saw as he was poised and ready to launch his RPG into Zebulon Batke's Humvee in Baghdad. He suddenly stopped in mid-action, stared at something, then shouted at his comrade, causing them both to turn and run for their lives (see testimony page 230).

We can all recall close calls in which we escaped a tragedy, yet there was no explanation in the natural. It is possible "to entertain angels without knowing it," as it says in Hebrews 13:2; but sadly, I believe most Christians have a tendency to disregard the ministry of angels altogether.

Several famous writers, including C. S. Lewis,[6] have alluded to the battle at Mons, Belgium, where a great number of British soldiers reported having seen what they all called an "intervention by angels" who came to their aid against the Germans in August 1914. According to the reports of these soldiers, this angelic assistance could not have come at a better moment, for they were being overrun by persistent German advancement.

A similar version of the Mons story was told by German prisoners who described what they called an "army of ghosts armed with bows and arrows and led by a very tall figure on a white horse who urged the English troops to go forward." Many diaries and letters show that, by 1915, the British had accepted the belief that a supernatural event had, indeed, taken place. Military historians who have studied this Belgium battle scene have enthusiastically incorporated the appearance of the angels at Mons into their writings.

In another account of the battle in Mons, some Coldstream Guards who were the last to withdraw had become lost in or near the Mormal Forest, and had dug in to make a last stand. An angel appeared and led them across an open field to a hidden, sunken road, which enabled them to escape. Truly England has had a long history of linking the heavenly to the military!

I would also like to relate a modern-day example involving someone we know personally. Floyd Bowers, a close friend of ours who worked in the mines of Clovis, New Mexico, had the responsibility of setting off the explosives. One particular day he was ready to push the switch when someone tapped him on the shoulder. To his surprise no one was anywhere around. Deciding it must have been his imagination, he prepared once again to detonate the dynamite when he felt another tap on his shoulder. Again, no one was there. Floyd decided to move all the ignition equipment several hundred feet back up the tunnel. When he finally plunged the charger, the whole top of the tunnel caved in exactly where he had been standing. A coincidence? You could never make our friend believe that. He knew *someone* had tapped him on the shoulder.

Are you in harm's way? Do you feel alone? You are not alone. He has assigned His angels—personal heavenly bodyguards—to protect you. There are more fighting *for* you than *against* you.

Verse 11 of Psalm 91 says, "For He will give His angels *charge* concerning you!" What does that mean? Think with me for a moment! Have you ever taken charge of a situation? When you take charge of something, you put yourself in a place of leadership. You begin telling everyone what to do and how to do it. If angels are taking charge of the things that concern us, God has given the angels, *not the circumstances*, the authority to act on our behalf. That same truth is repeated in Hebrews.

Are they [angels] not all ministering
spirits, sent out to render service for
the sake of those who will inherit
salvation? (Hebrews 1:14)

When we look to God as the source of our
protection and provision, the angels are constantly
rendering us aid and taking charge of our affairs.
Psalm 103:20 says, "His angels, mighty in strength...
[obey] the voice of His word!" As we proclaim God's
Word, the angels hasten to carry it out.

Verse 11 also says, "Angels will guard you in all
your ways." Have you ever seen a soldier standing
guard, protecting someone? That soldier stands at
attention: alert, watchful, and ready to protect at the
first sign of attack. How much more will God's angels
stand guard over God's children, alert and ready to
protect them at all times? Do we believe that? Have
we even thought about it? Faith is what releases this
promise to work in our behalf. How comforting it is
to know that God has placed these heavenly guards to
have charge over us.

Psalm 91 names many different avenues through
which God protects us. It is exciting to realize from
this Old Testament psalm that protection is not just a
random idea in God's mind. He is committed to it!

Angelic protection is another one of the unique
ways in which God has provided that protection.
What an unusual idea to add actual beings designed
to protect us. He has charged angels to guard us in all
our ways.

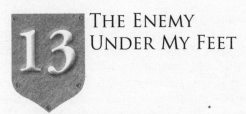

THE ENEMY UNDER MY FEET

You will tread upon the lion and cobra, the young lion and the serpent you will trample down.

—Psalm 91:13

Here in verse 13 God transitions to another topic. He takes us from the subject of our being protected by *Him* and puts emphasis on the *authority in His name* that has been given to us as believers.

Make a note of the corresponding New Testament Scripture dealing with the authority He has given to us:

> Behold, I [Jesus] have given you authority to tread on serpents and scorpions, and over all the power of the enemy, and nothing will injure you. (Luke 10:19)

We, as Christians, have been given authority over the enemy. *He does not have authority over us!* We need to take the time to allow that awesome reality to soak in. However, our authority over the enemy is not automatic.

My husband believes that too few Christians ever use their authority. Too often they *pray* when they should be *taking authority*! For the most part Jesus prayed at night and took authority all day. When we encounter the enemy is not the time to start praying. We need to be already "prayed up." *When we encounter the enemy* is when we need to speak forth the authority we have in the name of Jesus.

If a gunman suddenly faced you, would you be confident enough in your authority that you could boldly declare, "I am in covenant with the living God, and I have a blood covering that protects me from anything you might attempt to do; so in the name of Jesus, I command you to put down that gun"?

If we do not have that kind of courage, then we need to meditate on the authority Scriptures until we become confident in who we are *in Christ*. At new birth we immediately have enough power placed at our disposal to tread upon the enemy without being harmed. Most Christians, however, either do not know it or they fail to use it. How often do we believe the Word enough to act on it?

Now let's look at what this verse is actually saying. What good does it do to have authority over lions and cobras unless we are in Africa or India or someplace like that? What does it mean when it says we will tread on the lion, the young lion, the cobra, and the serpent (translated as "dragon" in the *King James Version*)? These words are graphic "representations" of things that are potentially harmful in our daily lives. They amount to *unforgettable ways* of describing the different types of satanic oppression that come against us. So, what do these terms mean to us today? Let's break them down.

1) First of all, we can encounter *lion problems.* These problems are bold, loud, and forthright and often come right out in

the open to hit us head-on. At one time or another we have all had something blatant and overt come against us. It might have been a car wreck or a face-to-face encounter with the enemy on the battlefield. It might have been an unexpected bill at the end of the month, causing a chain reaction of bounced checks. Those are *lion* problems—obvious difficulties that often seem insurmountable. Yet God says we will tread on *them*, and they will not tread on *us*.

2) The *young lions* are less obvious, smaller issues that can grow into full-scale problems if we don't handle them. Young lion problems come to harass and destroy us gradually, like little foxes. Subtle, negative thoughts that tell us we will not survive, or that our mate no longer loves us, or we no longer love our mate, are all good examples of this category. Small harassments, distractions, and irritations are young lions.

"Catch the foxes for us, the little foxes that are ruining the vineyards, while our vineyards are in blossom" (Song of Solomon 2:15).

"And those little foxes will grow into big ones if they are not taken captive and destroyed" (2 Corinthians 10:4–5). Answer those little foxes with the Word of God.

3) Next, God names *cobra* problems. These are the problems that seem to sneak up on us like snakes in the grass throughout the day. They are what we might call an undercover attack that brings sudden death—a deceptive scheme keeping us blinded until it devours us. A surprise military ambush, failure to distinguish the enemy from a civilian, a Dear John letter—these are all examples of cobra problems. Thank the Lord, we have authority to tread over such things, so they should never overpower us.

How many times have you seen a marriage unexpectedly fall apart, sometimes so suddenly you can't imagine what happened—only to find out later that underlying problems had been developing behind the scenes? By the time the cause was uncovered, the poison had had its effect. There is a lot of pressure on military marriages, and Satan's cobra attacks are behind most of those vulnerabilities—pornography, failure to keep the marriage bed holy, long periods of absence from the family. These things are hard to detect at first; they are similar to the puncture wounds from cobra fangs. Although no one sees the poison as it travels through a body, the results are always damaging, and often deadly. Only His restoration and forgiveness can undo those attacks once they have occurred.

4) We might have guessed at the previous examples, but what are *dragon* problems? I looked up the Hebrew word in *Strong's Concordance* and it listed *sea monster*. First of all, there is no such thing

as a dragon or a sea monster. Dragons are a figment of one's imagination. But have you ever experienced fears that were a figment of your imagination? Sure you have. We all have!

Dragon problems represent our unfounded, phantom, or mirage fears. That sounds harmless enough, but are you aware that phantom fears can be as deadly as reality fears, if we believe them?

Some people's *dragon* fears are as real to them as another person's *lion* problems. That's why it is so important to define your fears. So many people spend all of their lives running from something that is not even chasing them. Many people come home from combat and what was once a *lion* problem becomes a *phantom* problem they battle the rest of their lives.

"The wicked flee when no one is pursuing" (Proverbs 28:1).

This verse is a good definition of phantom fears. Many people have shared testimonies that speak of God's deliverance from things like *fear of the unknown, fear of facing the future alone, fear of loss, fear of death, tormenting suspicions,* and *claustrophobia*.

Dragon fear is a very valid form of spiritual attack, especially for soldiers who have been subjected to extended periods of intense battle. My daughter and her husband lived in an apartment when they first married. The apartment was managed by a Vietnam veteran. Angelia came up behind him one day to bring their rent check, and he went into "attack mode." Afterward he apologized profusely, but his body was still living in the past. He was out of danger but he was still dwelling there.

Others experience mental gymnastics and restless nights—rehearsing all the things that can go wrong in each situation. Dragon fears keep one living in the past or the future, rather than experiencing life in the present. Fantasy fears can cause us to do a lot of unnecessary running in life, so authority over dragons is not a mental game.

But, the *good news* is that God says we will tread on all of the powers of the enemy—no matter how loud and bold, sneaky and deceptive, or imaginary those powers might be. God has given us authority over all of them! No longer are we to put up with the paralyzing fears that at one time gripped our hearts and left us powerless. God has given us His power of attorney, and these problems now have to submit to the authority of His name.

I like that word *tread*. I think of a tank crossing a brushy plain. Where the tank treads go, everything is crushed and left flat on the ground. It is a great picture of our authority over these spiritual enemies as well, treading like a tank and crushing all that is evil in our path. That is a strong description of our authority in walking over the lion, the young lion, the cobra, and the dragon.

14 BECAUSE I LOVE HIM

Because he has loved Me, therefore I will... —Psalm 91:14

In verses 14 through 16 of Psalm 91, the author changes from talking in the third person *about* God's promises to God speaking to us personally from His secret place and *announcing* His promises in the first person.

It is a dramatic shift in tone as it moves to God speaking prophetically to each one of us directly, denoting significantly more depth in the relationship. In these three verses He gives seven promises, with as much obvious triumph as a man has when a woman accepts his proposal. A commitment to love involves choice. When you pick one person out of all others, you set your love on that one and embark on a deeper relationship. That is the picture of how God sets His love on us. Love is the cohesiveness that binds man to God, and God will be faithful to His beloved. Love always requires presence and nearness. Special memories are birthed out of relationship. That is why these verses cannot be fully explained, but must be experienced. Let me give you an illustration.

If you are a parent, you might have watched in horror as your young child picked up a newborn kitten by the throat and carried it all over the yard. You might have wondered how it ever survived.

For our family, it was an old, red hen that endured the distress dished out by our very enthusiastic children. Ole Red would allow herself to be picked up while in the process of laying her egg and would deposit it right in Angie's eager little hands. Truly there was some merit to the way the children advertised *the freshest eggs in town*—a few times the eggs never hit the nest!

Nesting season had its own special fascination for the children as they watched Ole Red try to hatch out more eggs than she could sit on. The kids would number the eggs in pencil to ensure that each egg was properly rotated and kept warm. They would wait out the twenty-one days, and then, with contagious delight, would call me out to see the nest swarming with little ones. That old hen had a brood of chicks that was hatched out of eggs from every hen in the henhouse.

Observing a setting hen this close had its own rare charm, as one could witness the *protection* she gave those chicks in a way most people never have the chance to observe. I remember her feathers as she fanned them out. I remember the smell of the fresh straw the kids kept in the nest. I remember that I could see through the soft, downy underside and watch the rhythmic beating of her heart. Those chicks had an almost enviable position—something all the books on the *theology of protection* could never explain in mere words. This was the unforgettable picture of a real-life understanding of what it means to be *under the wings*. Those were some happy chicks! True protection has everything to do with *closeness*.

Some people acknowledge that there is a God; others *know* Him. Neither maturity, nor education, nor family heritage, nor even a lifetime as a nominal Christian can make a person *"know"* Him. Only an encounter with the Lord and time spent with Him will cause one to lay hold of the promises in Psalm 91.

We need to ask ourselves, "Do I really love Him?" Jesus even asked this of Peter, a close disciple (see John 21:15). Can you imagine how Peter must have felt when Jesus asked three times, "Peter, do you love Me?"

Even so, we need to question ourselves, because these promises are made only to those who have genuinely set their love on Him. Take special note of the fact that *these seven promises are reserved for those who return His Love.*

And remember the Lord said in John 14:15: "If you love Me, you will keep My commandments." Our obedience is a reliable, telltale sign that shows we really love Him.

Do you love Him? If you do, *these promises are for you!*

GOD IS MY DELIVERER

Because he has loved Me, therefore I will deliver him.

—Psalm 91:14

A promise of deliverance is the first of the seven promises made to the one who loves God. Make it personal! For instance, I quote it like this: "Because I love You, Lord, I thank You for Your promise to deliver me."

When I was young I personally needed deliverance. I almost destroyed my marriage, my family, and my reputation because I was tormented with fear. One incident, while attempting to witness to a Buddhist girl without my having any knowledge of the spiritual warfare I would encounter, opened the door to evil. I can remember the very instant my happy life changed into a nightmare that lasted eight years. And one verse walked me out of this living mental hell: "Whoever calls on the name of the LORD will be delivered" (Joel 2:32). Many of you desperately need God's promise of deliverance. The Word worked for me and it will work for you.

There are also other types of deliverances, the internal and the external. Remember the external deliverances discussed in previous chapters; God will deliver us from *all* of the following:

- Lion problems
- Young lion problems
- Cobra problems
- Dragon problems
- Terror by night (evils that come through man: war, terror, violence)
- Arrows that fly by day (enemy assignments sent to wound)
- Pestilence (plagues, deadly diseases, fatal epidemics)
- Destruction (evils over which man has no control)

In other words, God wants to deliver us from every evil known to mankind. And that protection does not stop just because we might be on foreign soil, alone on a dangerous mission, or in the middle of a fierce battle. In his book *A Table in the Presence,* Lieutenant Carey Cash tells firsthand of our military's entry into Baghdad, and gives us eyewitness reports of the miraculous delivering power of our God.

> On April 10, 2003, the 1st Battalion, 5th Marine Regiment, marched into downtown Baghdad to seize Saddam Hussein's presidential palace, only to find themselves ambushed by militants hiding in mosques, storefronts, and homes. Hundreds of troops came face-to-face with a blitz of rocket-propelled grenades (RPGs), gunfire, and

sure defeat. Yet their reports tell a different story:

• A rocket splicing its way through an armored vehicle packed with Marines hits no one.

• A Marine finds a bullet's entrance and exit holes in his helmet, yet he has no injury.

• A squad of Marines watch in amazement as their enemies prepare to fire from point-blank range, then pause and drop their weapons, running away in terror.

• An RPG, fired from only a few yards away, inexplicably swerves and misses its intended target.

When the smoke of the battle cleared, only one American had lost his life. The Marines could not deny God's protection, not only on this day but in the months that led up to this moment as well. From a spiritual revival in the desert of Northern Kuwait, to miraculous escapes from death, to baptizing a Marine in Saddam Hussein's palace, Lieutenant Cash—a chaplain with the United States Navy and a battalion chaplain to infantry Marines, the first ground combat force to cross the border into Iraq—recounts the remarkable events, one

after another, of God's faithfulness.
(See testimony on page 226.)

Each war has its testimonies of deliverance.
Another fascinating story comes from an earlier war
in our history. Captain Edward W. Rickenbacker,
foremost American airman in World War II, was
thankful he knew to call on the name of the Lord
for deliverance. The remarkable story below,[7] written
soon after his return, describes a near-death experience
in which he was stranded in the South Pacific for
twenty-four days, on an ill-fated goodwill tour during
World War II.

> Captain Rickenbacker, ("flying
> ace" from WWI), left Hawaii by
> airplane with seven others for a
> certain island, but when their
> arrival time had elapsed, there was
> no land in sight. Their compass had
> failed them and their radio was not
> working properly. They were lost!
> And to make matters worse, their
> gas tank was empty, causing a crash
> landing into the water.
> The first miracle was the fact
> that this was probably the only
> time in history that a four-motor
> plane, designed to land only on
> the ground, had landed in the
> ocean without serious casualties.
> Water was pouring into the broken
> windows with such force that in
> their eagerness to get away from the

airplane before it sank they were unable to retrieve their drinking water and rations. All they had between them were four scrawny oranges. For eight days those eight men should have consumed a total of 192 meals, yet they subsisted on those four oranges and no water.

There were three rubber boats, two of which were designed to hold five men, but Rickenbacker's crew was sure that whoever had designed those rafts must have constructed them with midgets in mind. None of the men wanted to think about the fact that they had landed in an expanse of water covering over 68,000,000 square miles and enveloping more than a third of the globe. It accounts for half the world's water surface and is 11 million square miles greater than the total land surface of 57,510,000 square miles. How on earth could three tiny rubber rafts be seen in that great expanse?

There were no comfortable positions. A standard position, but most awkward, was one man's legs over another man's shoulders and the other man's legs under the other man's arms.

Twelve-foot-high waves turned one of the rafts over and no sooner had the occupants gotten it upright and pulled themselves back inside than they all noticed the water was suddenly churning alive with sharks. They could see their dark bodies circling their rafts throughout the whole ordeal. During the day the sun would burn them beyond belief, yet they would almost freeze during the cold nights.

The lifeboats were tied together with three men in the first one, three in the second (including Captain Rickenbacker), and two in the third. Private Bartek in Captain Rickenbacker's boat had a Bible in the pocket of his jumper and the second day out prayer meetings were organized in the evening and morning and the men took turns reading passages from the Bible. They laid bear their inmost secrets and sins to God, none of which will ever be revealed. There were some cynics and unbelievers among them—not after the eighth day, however. For on that day a small miracle occurred. Something landed on Rickenbacker's head!

Rickenbacker said "Frankly and humbly we prayed for deliverance and if it weren't for the fact I had seven witnesses, I wouldn't dare tell this next story because it seems so fantastic. Within an hour after the prayer meeting on the eighth day, a seagull came out of nowhere and landed on my head. I reached up my hand very gently and got him. We wrung his neck, defeathered him, carved up his carcass into eight equal pieces, divided it among the group and ate every bite—even the little bones."

Rickenbacker said, "Our spirits rose...all because of one little gull hundreds of miles from land. And there was not a one of us who was not aware that our gull had appeared just after we finished our prayer service (which we held twice a day). After our feast, we then used his innards for bait. With this bait we succeeded in catching two fish.

"That night we ran into our first rainstorm. Usually you try to avoid a black squall, but in this case we made it our business to get into it and catch water for drinking. Later we were able to catch more water and build up a supply." Rickenbacker said, "Added to my physical effort were my prayers. I had asked God to help us paddle to reach the storm so we could catch fresh water." It was nothing short of a miracle that they were able to maneuver those rubber boats that far by nightfall. Then they busied themselves catching water with their shirts, socks, and handkerchiefs and wringing them out. Even when one of the boats capsized, they learned that determined men who won't give up can do anything. In the midst of all the turbulence, the other rafts were able to rescue the sunken one and help the men back in to safety.

Rickenbacker, who had started that journey with a message to deliver to General MacArthur, said that it was clear that God had a purpose in keeping him alive. He knew he had been saved to serve. He had faced death and had learned from those encounters the meaning of life, the meaning of God, and the meaning of the Golden Rule.

During the last days their supply of water increased and on the twenty-fourth day American planes found and rescued Captain Rickenbacker and his men. Finally, after what seemed like a lifetime, Rickenbacker was able to transport the oral message he had been commissioned to deliver to General MacArthur—a message that will forever remain a secret. Rickenbacker said, "Though I remember every word of it to this day, I shall not repeat it. Stimson and MacArthur took it with them to the grave, and so shall I."

The survival of the airmen was important to the war effort in other ways. Because of the experiences of those eight men, survival equipment was redesigned. Life rafts were made longer and wider, carried sails and such emergency supplies as concentrated food, vitamins, first-aid kits, fishing tackle, and bait. They were also fitted with radios and with small chemical distillers capable of converting seawater into drinking water.

But beyond helping the war effort, the experiences of the rescued airmen had far-reaching spiritual results. They made powerful witnessing Christians of the airmen who had experienced the miraculous answers to their prayers, and through them made a strong impression upon the American public.

Equally outspoken about his experiences on the raft in the Pacific Ocean was Johnny Bartek: "Then we prayed and God answered. It was real. We needed water. We prayed for water and we got water—all we needed. Then we asked for fish, and we got fish. And we got some meat when we prayed. Seagulls don't go around sitting on people's heads waiting to be caught.... Then I prayed again to God and said, 'If You'll send that one plane back for us, I promise I'll believe in You and tell everyone else.' That plane came back and the others flew on. It just happened? It did not! God sent that plane back!"

The whole free world was thrilled by the rescue and by Captain Rickenbacker's words: "We prayed, and we were spared to come back and tell America to pray."

Deliverance is all-encompassing. It happens within (internal) and without (external); in fact, it surrounds us.

You are my hiding place; You preserve me from trouble; You surround me with songs of deliverance. (Psalm 32:7)

I AM SEATED ON HIGH

Because he has loved Me…I will set him securely on high, because he has known my name. —Psalm 91:14

To be set securely on high is the second promise to those who love the Lord and know Him by name. "It is My Name," God says, "that has been on his lips when he faces troubles, and he has run to Me. He has called out to Me in faith; therefore, I will set him on high."

> …which He brought about in Christ, when He raised Him from the dead and seated Him at His right hand in the heavenly places, far above all rule and authority and power and dominion, and every name that is named, not only in this age but also in the one to come… and raised us up with Him, and seated us with Him in the heavenly places in Christ Jesus. (Ephesians 1:20–21; 2:6)

It is interesting that God pulls us up to where He is! Things look better from higher up. Our vantage point is much improved when we are seated with Him on high.

Hebrews 8:11 quotes Jeremiah speaking of the New Covenant to come and comparing it to the Old Testament, in effect saying, "They will no longer say, '*Know (Strong's Concordance:* to have knowledge of*)* the Lord'." Most people under the Old Testament, according to Jeremiah, only had knowledge *about* God—they just had an *acquaintance* with Him. However, the writer uses a different word ("*know*") in the same verse to describe our knowledge of God under the New Covenant.

The second time the word *know* is used in Hebrews 8:11, according to *Strong's Concordance*, it means "to stare at, discern clearly, to experience or to gaze with wide open eyes as though gazing at something remarkable." When God refers to our knowing Him today, He is referring to something much more personal than what people experienced during the Old Testament.

Recently I was watching a WWII documentary and one of the veterans interviewed made the comment, "There was a lot more cursing going on than the movie depicted." If you struggle with using God's name in vain, meditate on this verse about the use of God's name. Jesus tells us in Mark 9:39, "There is no one who shall perform a miracle in My name, and be able soon afterward to speak evil of Me." It is so important to realize that the Name you call on can save you. It can set you securely on high. Or, you can use the name and speak evil which gives no help to your situation. It makes no sense to have access to the Name who can work miracles and deliver your life and not use it in a way that renders you mercy. Many times we lose spiritual battles with our mouths and we open ourselves up for assaults. An environment of cursing opens the door for being cursed, yet calling on God for help renders aid. When you get a revelation of the power of that Name it not only causes you to refrain from evil but it gives you a reverence for Him, just as you would respect the name of one of your close friends. I challenge you to meditate on God's promise, "I will set him on high because He has known My Name." These are not just empty words.

This promise of being seated securely on high is for the one who experiences God intimately. Read this verse in first person. "Lord, You have promised You will set me securely on high because I have known Your name on a firsthand basis. I have experienced Your covenant promises described in Your different covenant names."

In the first two sentences of Psalm 91 alone, the writer refers to God by four different names, progressively denoting stronger relationship. The writer refers to God as *the Most High,* revealing that He is the highest thing that exists. This implies so much more significance when we realize that *we are set securely on high* with the One who is Most High. From on high we have a better vantage point and better perspective.

In the opening of Psalm 91 God is also called the *Almighty,* denoting that He is "all" mighty—the most powerful. Next he is referred to as *The Lord,* revealing ownership. Then he calls Him *My God,* making it personal. We see God unveiled in four unique ways to the man who has known His name.

Verse 14 introduces two conditions and two promises that link back to the beginning of the psalm—*because he has loved Me* and *because he has known My name*—each introduced with the word *because* to catch our attention. Then He responds with two promises of deliverance and positioning. We love the fact that God faithfully keeps His promises, but have we kept ours? This next story reminds us of how important it is to keep our promises to God.

A number of soldiers in Iowa's 113th Cavalry—an outfit that fought superbly in the European war—received Easter cards that opened their eyes. The front of the card included a sketch of a German battlefield labeled *Easter, 1945*. On top was the word *Remember?* in large letters. On the inside of the card was a family fireside sketch and the following: "Well, God DID what you asked! He delivered you safely home and set you back on high. Now! Have you done what you promised? How about Easter, 1950?"

The card was signed by the Reverend Ben L. Rose, pastor of the Central Presbyterian Church in Bristol, Virginia. This pastor knew their promises—he had been the chaplain of the 113th Cavalry.

Many times in dangerous situations we make God promises—foxhole commitments. What a reminder! Do we sincerely love Him? This chaplain wanted to make sure his men remembered their vows.

Do we really know Him by name and trust in His promises? Have we been faithful to keep the promises we've made to Him?

GOD ANSWERS MY CALL

He will call upon Me, and I will answer him.

—Psalm 91:15

God makes a third promise here in verse 15, that He will *answer* those who truly love Him and call on His name. Are we aware of what a wonderful promise God is making to us here?

> This is the confidence which we have before Him, that, if we ask anything according to His will, He hears us. And if we know He hears us in whatever we ask, we know that we have the requests which we asked from Him. (1 John 5:14–15)

Nothing gives me more comfort than to realize that, every time I request something in prayer, if I pray in line with God's Word, He hears me. And if He hears me I know I will have a response, even if I might not understand it immediately. This one promise keeps me continually searching His Word, to understand His will and His promises so I can know how to pray more effectively. Sometimes I just cry out to God for help.

During one of our floods several years ago, our son Bill had a herd of goats on some land by the bayou. As the bayou water began to rise and overflow its banks, some men saw Bill's goats being overtaken by the flood and hoisted them up into the loft of a barn to keep them from drowning.

By the next morning the water was like a rushing river—a mile wide—washing away uprooted trees and everything else in its path. Bill had, by this time, been told about his goats, and in spite of the roadblocks and the rapids gushing by, he set out in an old tin-bottom boat across those swift floodwaters to rescue his little herd of goats. He knew in another few hours they would die from thirst and suffocation.

Little Willie was the most precious of all the herd because of the time Bill had spent bottle-feeding him. The cry of that little goat was the first Bill heard when he got close to the barn. And as you might expect, once Bill forced the loft door open amid the rushing waters, Little Willie was the first to jump into his arms. Then, boatload by boatload, goat by goat, Bill got every one of those animals out of the loft and rowed them to safety.

A television camera crew from Abilene, while filming the flood, caught sight of the little goat boy risking his life to rescue his goats. That became the news story of the day, making the broadcast at six o'clock and again at ten. That is a heartwarming story, but every time I think of Bill rescuing those goats in trouble, I think of how merciful God is to answer us when we sincerely call to Him for help.

As important as individual praying is, nothing seems to compare to a nation praying in faith. When English soldiers were trapped at Dunkirk—with the

German army behind them and the English Channel in front of them—the prime minister warned the nation that no more than twenty or thirty thousand of the two hundred thousand British soldiers could possibly be rescued from those exposed beaches. But no one could have estimated the power of a nation in prayer. The churches of England were filled—while the king and queen knelt at Westminster Abby, the Archbishop of Canterbury, the Prime Minister, the Cabinet, the good Wilhelmina, and members of parliament were all on their knees.

1) Suddenly, one of the Nazi generals decided to regroup and ordered a halt of the German troops when they were only twelve miles away from Dunkirk. Hitler then made a rash decision to hold them there indefinitely.

2) The weather suddenly proved to be a great hindrance to the enemy planes firing on the English, who appeared to be trapped like mice on that French coast.

3) Instantly, every imaginable vessel that would float—everything from private boats piloted by bank clerks, fishermen, Boy Scouts, yachtsmen, barge operators, college professors, and tugboat captains started their rescue mission. Even London fire brigade boats got in on the action. Shipyards were quickly

set up to repair vessels that were
damaged, so they could return for
another load.

Anyone would have said the undertaking was
absurd, but the *prayers of a nation* strengthened the
people in one of the most dangerous and seemingly
impossible endeavors in all of history.

On the boats taking them to safety, the men began
to pray—many of whom had never prayed before. At
the camps in England the men requested permission
to pray. It became apparent to all of Britain that their
prayers were being heard. Over 7,000 troops were
evacuated the first day; 47,310 the second day; then
53,823, 68,014, and 64,429 in the next three days,
and so on through the following days and nights. In
the final total, 338,000 British, Belgian, and French
troops were brought to safety.

Beyond that, collective prayers were being called
for on both sides of the ocean at strategic turning
points of the war. President Franklin Roosevelt from
America issued a proclamation for prayer and a nation
responded. America had its problems, not only in
Europe, but also on her western flank in the Pacific
War Theater. Mayor LaGuardia called the whole city
of New York to pray when Captain Rickenbacker and
his men radioed their last message on October 22,
1942: "May have overshot island. Hour's fuel." After
twenty-four suspenseful days, Eddie Rickenbacker
and his companions were rescued out of their
hopeless nightmare in the Pacific Ocean. And, having
experienced the power of prayer, all of those men were
moved to become strong witnessing Christians. What
tremendous testimonies to the might of the combined

prayers of the masses! When we think of the power of individual prayer, let's not forget history's record of what happens by the power of corporate prayer—it strengthens the individual's prayer.

When soldiers call upon God, He answers. When nations call upon God, history records it!

18 GOD RESCUES ME FROM TROUBLE

I will be with him in trouble; I will rescue him.

—Psalm 91:15

The fourth promise—to *rescue from trouble* those who love the Lord—is found in the middle of verse 15. It is a well-known fact that our human natures cry out to God when we are faced with trouble. Men in prison, soldiers in war, people in accidents—all seem to call out to God when they get in a crisis. Even atheists are known to call on the *God they don't acknowledge* when they are extremely afraid.

A lot of criticism has been leveled against those kinds of *court of last resort* prayers. However, in defense of this kind of praying, we must remember when one is in pain, he usually runs to the one he loves the most and the one he trusts. The alternative is not calling out at all, so this verse acknowledges that calling out to God in trouble is a good place for a person to start!

If a person has never felt threatened he might never think about needing protection. It is the one who knows he is in imminent danger who will appreciate and take the words of this psalm to heart. Military personnel, of all people, seem to be faced with more critical dangers than most, but God has a great deal of variety in His plentiful means of protection and modes of rescue from trouble.

This verse also reminds me of a story I read about a U.S. senator living in pre–Civil War days, a story said to be true. The senator had taken his son to the slave market, where the boy noticed a black mother crying and praying as traders were preparing to sell her daughter on the slave block. As he walked closer, he overheard the mother crying out, "Oh, God, if I could help You as easily as You could help me, I'd do it for You, Lord." The young man was so touched by the prayer he went over and bought the girl off the slave block and gave her back to her mother.

God answers our prayers and rescues us in so many different ways. I am so thankful He is creative and not hindered by our seemingly impossible situations. But we have to ask in faith and not confine Him to our limited resources. God says, "If you love Me, I will be with you when you find yourself in trouble, and I will rescue you." But we have to trust Him to do it His way.

British newspapers told of a British submarine in WWII that lay helpless on the ocean floor and needed to be rescued. After two days, hope of raising her was abandoned. The crew, on orders of the commanding officer, began singing:

> Abide with me! Fast falls the
> eventide, the darkness deepens—
> Lord, with me abide! When other
> helpers fail and comforts flee, Help
> of the helpless, oh, abide with me![8]

The officer explained to the men that they did not have long to live. There was no hope of outside aid because the surface searchers did not know the vessel's position. Sedative pills were distributed to the men to quiet their nerves.

However, one sailor was affected more quickly than the others, and he fainted. In doing so he fell against a piece of equipment and set in motion the submarine's jammed surfacing mechanism. Crying out to God delivered these men when there was no hope, and God used something as simple as a hymn and a pill to get this submarine back to the surface and safely to the port.

> When you pass through the waters,
> I will be with you; and through the
> rivers, they will not overflow you.
> When you walk through the fire,
> you will not be scorched, nor will
> the flame burn you. (Isaiah 43:2)

Our son, Bill, once saw the rescuing power of God when he found himself in serious trouble after attempting to swim across a lake that was much wider than he had calculated. With no strength left in his body, and having already gone under twice, Bill experienced all the sensations of drowning. But miraculously, God not only provided a woman on the opposite bank, which had been deserted, but also enabled her to throw a life ring (that just happened to be near) more than thirty yards, landing within inches of his almost lifeless body.

Although some people might call happenings like

these a coincidence, the negative situations that we encounter can become *God-incidences* when we trust His Word. That was certainly Bill's day of trouble, but I thank God He was with Bill, and rescued him.

GOD HONORS ME

I will…honor him. —Psalm 91:15

The fifth promise—to honor those who love God—is in the last part of verse 15. All of us like to be honored. I can remember when the teacher called my name while I was in grade school, and complimented my work on a paper I'd turned in. That thrilled me. I was honored.

Several years ago our daughter, Angelia, attended a political rally in our city that was given for George W. Bush when he was campaigning for governor. She had shared a quick anecdote with him at the beginning of the meeting when they first met. After he had spoken to the group and was leaving with some of his colleagues, everyone was shocked when he left his group and darted back to our daughter to say, "Remember the promise I made—no tears for you in November!"

She had told him that she would not be able to hold back the tears if he lost the election. It honored her that he not only remembered her but also recalled their conversation.

When this book was written, our granddaughter's husband, Heath Adams, was a staff sergeant in the U.S. Air Force. He recently finished Airman Leadership School and was then stationed at Great Falls, Montana.

We were all thrilled when he received the John Levitow Award, the highest award given at the leadership school banquet. It was not only an honor for him, but it was also an honor for his whole squadron. Then he was one of eight people chosen from 4,500 security forces to represent Air Force Space Command in the Defender Challenge Competition where his team took silver medals in the obstacle course and tactics events, placing second overall.

Heath was also a distinguished graduate at Security Force Level II Combat Leaders Course. He won the Air Force SF Noncommissioned Officer Award at 20th Air Force and had the honor of giving a warrior brief to the secretary of the Air Force—the first warrior brief the secretary had ever heard. The commander coordinated a surprise ceremony to give Heath his promotion, and secretly arranged for our granddaughter, Jolena, to be there. Not only was his military service noted, but his character as a family man, a youth pastor, and, ultimately, a faithful follower of Christ, evidenced in his activity with a local church, was communicated to the group. The ceremony honored Heath before all his peers.

Men have many types of customs to honor other men, from ceremonies and speeches to medals of distinction. I have had the highest admiration for each serviceman I've interviewed as they showed me their Purple Hearts and their Medals of Honor. Those are symbols of the honors that have been bestowed on those recipients.

Not only is it an honor, but it feels good to have someone we consider important pay special attention to us. However, even though it is a distinct thrill to be honored by man, how much more of a tribute and a thrill do we experience when we are honored by God? Fulfilling our part of the Covenant allows God to honor us.

Have you ever thought about what it means to be honored by the God of the universe? He honors us by calling us His sons and daughters. He honors us by answering when we take His Word seriously and call out to Him in faith. He honors us by recognizing us individually and by preparing a place for us to be with Him eternally.

Giving us honor is one of the seven unique, bonus promises God made to us in Psalm 91.

20 GOD SATISFIES ME WITH LONG LIFE!

With a long life I will satisfy him. —Psalm 91:16

The sixth promise of the final verses of Psalm 91 is found in verse sixteen. God does not only say that He will prolong our lives and give us a lot of birthdays. No! He says He will *satisfy* us with a long life. There are people who would testify that simply having a great many birthdays is not necessarily a blessing. But God says He will give us many birthdays, and as those birthdays roll around we will experience satisfaction.

It has been said that there is a God-shaped vacuum inside each of us. Man has tried to fill that vacuum with many different things, but nothing will satisfy the emptiness until it is filled with Jesus. He is the true satisfaction to which God refers in His promise.

God is making the offer. If we will come to Him, let Him fill that empty place on the inside, and allow Him to help us fulfill the call on our lives, then He will give us a long life and satisfy us as we live it out. Only the dissatisfied person can really appreciate what it means to find satisfaction.

It is a fact that God wants us to live a satisfied life, but let's not neglect the promise of a long life. King David was Israel's most valiant, daring warrior, yet he lived to a ripe old age—*full of days*, as the Old Testament authors liked to say. His life was filled with combat, high-risk situations, and impossible odds. Yet he did not die in battle; his head went down in peace in his old age. Long life is a great concluding promise of protection.

Paul lets us know in Ephesians that we are in a fight. We can't flow with what feels good and win this battle because the enemy will make the wrong path extremely easy to take.

Eddie Rickenbacker, the World War I flying ace, once wanted to let himself die but later said this about death: "I felt the presence of death, and I knew that I was going. You may have heard that dying is unpleasant, but don't you believe it. Dying is the sweetest, tenderest, most sensuous sensation I have ever experienced. Death comes disguised as a sympathetic friend. All was serene; all was calm. How wonderful it would be simply to float out of this world. It is easy to die. You have to fight to live. And that is what I did. I recognized that wonderful, mellow sensation for what it was—death—and I fought it. I literally fought death in my mind, pushing away the sweet blandishments and welcoming back the pain. The next ten days were a continuous fight with the old Grim Reaper, and again and again, I would feel myself start to slip away. Each time I rallied and fought back, until I had turned the corner toward recovery."

Captain Rickenbacker should know! Death came toward him many times in his service as a soldier in both world wars, when he survived two plane crashes and when he was lost for twenty-four days on the Pacific Ocean.

Sometimes the spirit of death makes a bid for our very life. It is these inner dynamics that are at work when a person is wounded, facing a serious illness, racked by pain from an injury, or sensing impending doom. It is easy to give in to it. We think of the ugly side of destruction, but the most danger arises when it comes with a pretty face. It is a fight to break free from the enticing call of death, persevere to victory, and redeem the covenant promise of a satisfied, long life.

Once, in a boat on the Sea of Galilee, the disciples cried out, fearing they would drown in the storm. Jesus, however, had said they must go to the other side. If they had thought through what He'd said, they would have known the storm would not harm them because they had His word concerning a mission across the lake. In the same way, if you have been promised a satisfying, long life, then you know you will make it through the present circumstances.

John Evans, a Welsh preacher, told of an incident that happened to his friend during the Civil War, soon after he received a captain's commission. Even though many of the men in the army had little regard for religion, it was fashionable for each soldier to carry a Bible.

While following orders to burn a fort, the captain and his men came under very heavy fire from the enemy. When the conflict was over, he found that a musket ball had lodged itself in his Bible, which was in his pocket. Had it not been for this intervention, he most assuredly would have been killed.

Investigating further, he then discovered that the bullet had come to rest on the verse Ecclesiastes 11:9, "Rejoice, O young man, in thy youth...walk in the ways of thine heart, and in the sight of thine eyes: but know thou, that for all these things God will bring thee into judgment" (KJV). This message made as deep an impression on his mind as did the way it was delivered. As a non-religious man, he realized the Bible had literally done more than just attempt to save his soul. As a result, he immediately turned his heart toward God and continued to be devout in his Christian walk to a good, old age. He often testified how the Bible became, that day, both the salvation of his body, as well as his soul.[9]

God was not interested only in protecting and extending this man's life—He was more interested in his faithful obedience as he lived *out* that life. In the same way, God wants us to claim the promise of long life, but He also wants us to use our long life living for Him.

Ask yourself, "What *am* I going to do with my long life?"

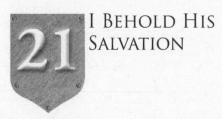

21 I BEHOLD HIS SALVATION

...and let him see My salvation. —Psalm 91:16

Allowing those who love Him to *behold His salvation* is the seventh promise in Psalm 91, found in the last part of verse 16. God wants us to take hold of His salvation.

The movement of this last line in Psalm 91 describes our ultimate, final victory. The order of this sentence gives us the promise that we will see salvation face-to-face *during and after* our long, satisfied life. This moves us beyond an intellectual knowledge of salvation, all the way to relationship.

It secures our future but it starts now! Jesus constantly reminded us, "Salvation is now! Today it has come!" Many people are surprised when they look up the word "*salvation*" in a Bible concordance and find it has a much deeper meaning than just *a ticket to heaven*. We often miss the richness of this promise.

According to *Strong's Concordance,* the word *salvation* includes health, healing, rescue, deliverance, safety, protection, and provision. What more could we ask? God promises He will allow us to see and *take hold of* His health, His healing, His deliverance, His protection, and His provision!

Many people read Psalm 91 and simply see it with their eyes, but very few *behold* it in their lives.

My prayer is for that to change for you. One of my biggest thrills comes when people write or call after I've taught this truth, and they describe the ecstatic joy of having it come alive in their heart. I love to hear the extent to which they have actually *taken hold of* this covenant and started experiencing it as a vital part of their existence.

You can be in the midst of a forsaken land with the enemy all around you, and you can still behold the salvation of the Lord. Many have actually experienced the sensation of the presence of the Lord in the midst of chaos. In the testimonies that follow, your heart will be encouraged by those who have beheld firsthand the salvation of the Lord.

Read their stories in their own words. The truth about God's salvation—His protection, deliverance, health, and provision—is more than just wishful thinking. It is a *promise* of which one can actually *take hold!*

In Summary

Nothing in this world is more reliable than God's promises, when we believe them, refuse to waver, and make His Word *our final authority* for every area of life.

There is, however, a uniqueness about this psalm. Promises of protection can be found throughout the Bible, but Psalm 91 is the only place in the Word where all of the protection promises are brought together in one collection—forming a covenant written through the Holy Spirit. How powerful that is!

I believe Psalm 91 is a covenant—a spiritual

contract that God has made available to His children. It is desperately needed in these difficult days. There are some who sincerely ask, "How do you know you can take a song from the psalms and base your life on it?"

Jesus answered that question. The value of the psalms was emphasized when He cited them as a source of truth that must be fulfilled:

> Now He said to them, "These are My words which I spoke to you while I was still with you, that all things which are written about Me in the Law of Moses and the Prophets *and the Psalms* must be fulfilled." (Luke 24:44, emphasis added)

When Jesus specifically equates the Psalms to the Law of Moses and the Prophets, we see that it is historically relevant, prophetically sound, and totally applicable and reliable.

At a time when there are so many uncertainties facing us, especially in the military, it is more than comforting to realize that God not only knows ahead of time what we will be facing but also makes absolute provision for us.

Someone once pointed out, "It is interesting that the world must have gotten its distress 911 number from God's answer to our distress call—Psalm 91:1."

It seems only a dream now to think back to the time when my mind was reeling in fears and doubts. Little did I know when I asked God that pertinent question—"Is there any way for a Christian to escape all the evils that are coming on this world?"—He was going to give me a dream that would not only change my life, but also change the lives of thousands of others who would hear and believe.

What Must I Do to Be Saved?

We've talked about physical protection. Now let's make sure that you have eternal protection. The promises from God in this book are for God's children who love Him. If you have never given your life to Jesus and accepted Him as your Lord and Savior, there is no better time than right now.

> There is none righteous, not even one. (Romans 3:10)

> For all have sinned and fall short of the glory of God. (Romans 3:23)

God loves you and gave His life that you might live eternally with Him.

> But God demonstrates His own love toward us, in that while we were yet sinners, Christ died for us. (Romans 5:8)

> For God so loved the world [you], that He gave His only begotten Son, that whoever believes in Him shall not perish, but have eternal life. (John 3:16)

There is nothing we can do to earn our salvation or to make ourselves good enough to go to heaven. It is a free gift!

> For the wages of sin is death, but
> the free gift of God is eternal life in
> Christ Jesus. (Romans 6:23)

There is also no other avenue through which we can reach heaven other than Jesus Christ—God's Son.

> "And there is salvation in no one
> else; for there is no other name
> under heaven that has been given
> among men by which we must be
> saved." (Acts 4:12)

> Jesus said to him, "I am the way,
> and the truth, and the life; no one
> comes to the Father but through
> Me." (John 14:6)

You must believe that Jesus is the Son of God, that He died on the cross for your sins, and that He rose again on the third day.

> ...[Jesus] was declared the Son of
> God with power by the resurrection
> from the dead. (Romans 1:4)

You may be thinking, *How do I accept Jesus and become His child?* God in His love has made it so easy.

> If you confess with your mouth
> Jesus as Lord, and believe in your
> heart that God raised Him from the
> dead, you will be saved. (Romans
> 10:9)

But as many as received Him, to them He gave the right to become children of God, even to those who believe in His name. (John 1:12)

It is as simple as praying a prayer similar to this one—if you sincerely mean it in your heart:

Dear God:

I believe You gave Your Son, Jesus, to die for me. I believe He shed His blood to pay for my sins and that You raised Him from the dead so I can be Your child and live with You eternally in heaven. I am asking Jesus to come into my heart right now and save me. I confess Him as the Lord and Master of my life.

I thank You, dear Lord, for loving me enough to lay down Your life for me. Take my life now and use it for Your glory. I ask for all that You have for me.

In Jesus' name,
Amen

Personal Psalm 91 Covenant

Copy and enlarge this Psalm 91 covenant prayer to pray over yourself or your loved one—inserting his or her name in blanks.

_____ dwells in the shelter of the Most High and (he/she) _____ abides in the shadow of the Almighty. _____ says to the Lord, "My refuge and my fortress, My God, in whom I trust!" For it is God who delivers _____ from the snare of the trapper and from the deadly pestilence (fatal, infectious disease). God will cover _____ with His pinions, and under His wings _____ may seek refuge; God's faithfulness is a shield and bulwark.

_____ will not be afraid of the terror by night, or of the arrow that flies by day; of the pestilence that stalks in darkness, or of the destruction that lays waste at noon. A thousand may fall at _____'s side, and 10,000 at (his/her) right hand; but it shall not approach _____. _____ will only look on with _____ eyes, and see the recompense of the wicked. For _____ has made the Lord, his/her refuge, even the Most High, _____ dwelling place. No evil will befall _____, nor will any plague come near _____'s tent. For He will give His angels charge concerning _____ to guard _____ in all his/her ways. They will bear _____ up in their hands, lest _____ strike his/her foot against a stone. _____ will tread upon the lion and cobra, the young lion and the serpent he/she will trample down.

Because _____ has loved Me (God said),

therefore I will deliver him/her; I will set _____ securely on high, because _____ has known My name. _____ will call on Me, and I will answer _____. I will be with _____ in trouble; I will rescue _____ and honor _____. With a long life I will satisfy _____, and let him/her behold My salvation.

Author's Note: *Some have been quite creative in writing their personal covenant. One soldier fighting in Vietnam wrote out his Psalm 91 declaration. His platoon always said, "Somewhere in the war there is a bullet out there with your name on it." So he prayed this specialized confession of deliverance:*

- Arrow = the bullet with my name on it
- Pestilence that stalks in darkness = the Viet Cong
- Snare of the trapper = booby traps and land mines
- 1000 will fall = open combat

Psalm 91 Testimonies

STORIES THAT DEMAND
TO BE TOLD

John Marion Walker
Army Air Corps Private 4th Class
Specialist 35th Air Group,
21st Pursuit Squadron
Survivor of the Bataan Death March

We all remember the brutal attack on
December 7, 1941, when Japanese torpedo bombers
devastated U.S. Navy ships stationed at Pearl Harbor
in the Hawaiian Islands, crippling almost every ship
and airplane in the U.S. Pacific fleet and giving
Japan temporary control of the Pacific. This initiated
America's involvement in WWII.

What many Americans do not remember,
however, is that on the very same day of the attack
on Pearl Harbor, the Japanese dropped bombs on
U.S. and Filipino troops stationed in the Philippines,
destroying their planes as well as their airfields. Nichols
Field in Manila was totally wiped out. With the U.S.
Air and Naval fleet badly crippled in Pearl Harbor, it
left the troops in the Philippines without aid.

John Walker was among the Americans who had

been sent to the Philippines, where he witnessed the latter attack. John had accepted Jesus as his Savior years before, but was not walking closely with the Lord at the time of the war. He had an older brother back home, however, who was a pastor and who was standing firm and immovable in faith that his younger brother, John, would, in fact, return home from the war. John recalled numerous instances where he knew God had intervened on his behalf to save his life. Thank God for family members who pray unwaveringly for the protection of loved ones!

One of these divine interventions took place during that early attack at Manila. The U.S. troops were living in tents under bamboo thickets. John was lying on his cot while a buddy was digging a foxhole several feet away.

"Three times he called my name," John recalled, "so, on the third time I left my cot and walked over to see what he needed. Surprisingly, he insisted he had not once called me. But before we had time to finish our conversation, a bomb hit the very cot on which I had been lying. From that moment on I knew God was with me."

In spite of being terribly outnumbered, outgunned, and without adequate supplies, these troops fought courageously to hold off the Japanese to the bitter end, but they were ultimately overpowered. It was during these early days of war, when Japan attacked for no apparent reason, that hatred for the Japanese started building in John's heart—a hate that grew increasingly until some fifty years later.

John remembers he was sent to Manila to handle the machine guns on P-40 aircraft, but instead, he found himself using an M-1 rifle with the Filipino 77th infantry on the front lines. Tokyo Rose aided the

Japanese military by taunting and demoralizing the American troops via radio, reminding them of their helpless situation and impending doom. According to John, some found her somewhat entertaining but to others, she was demoralizing.

During this time, another fateful God intervention happened when John was told to drive a truck to the front lines. He could have chosen from two trucks—a right-hand drive and a left-hand drive. He got into the left-hand drive because he was accustomed to it. But something told him, "John, don't take this truck," so he turned off the motor and jumped into the other truck. As soon as he entered the highway, gunfire went through the left side of the truck, exactly where he would have been sitting had he taken the other truck. Again, John realized God had spared him a second time.

The troops were forced to use World War I guns and ammunition that half the time didn't even work. Only one of four grenades exploded, and six of seven mortar rounds detonated. Many times corroded shells would burst the barrels of cannons. On the other hand, the Japanese were constantly being re-supplied with fresh troops, equipment, and food.

Yet despite Japan's advantage, the American and Filipino troops continued to fight, even though they lived on one-fourth rations, once a day for almost five months. This extended conflict, against impossible odds, bought much needed time for the rebuilding of the Pacific Fleet for our U.S. offensive in the Pacific. But on April 3, 1942, the Japanese surrounded them, and having been weakened to the point of total exhaustion these American and Filipino troops could no longer withstand the horrible onslaught of the enemy and were forced to surrender six days later.

This was the largest single defeat of American armed forces in history and it came, not from the wishes of more than 75,000 fighting soldiers who were ready to fight to the death, but from command orders, delivered in some cases under threat of court martial for failure to comply. On April 10, these 75,000 prisoners were lined up four abreast and started on a forced march that took place under the most brutal conditions imaginable.

Today that march is referred to as the *Bataan Death March*. They marched day and night without stopping, with no food or water from the Japanese, in very humid 115-degree temperatures. During this march John's new boots were worn completely out and he was barefoot for the remainder of his three-and-a-half-year imprisonment. The soldiers were never issued any more clothing, and before it was over his clothes had actually rotted off his body.

The Japanese would drive beside many of the troops, cutting off heads with their bayonets as they passed by. Some of the men were pushed in front of oncoming trucks—others were clubbed with the captors gun butts. At night, Filipinos would throw them stalks of sugar cane to chew on for strength. They also threw Poncit—something like bread made of rice mixed with bees, pork, and grasshoppers. The prisoners would break off chunks and then pass it on when the guards weren't looking. If these Filipino citizens had been caught they would have been killed.

The march never stopped, but the men discovered they could walk in their sleep. At night the two guys on the outside would lock arms with the two in the middle and let them sleep. Then, when the guards were not watching, they would change places so the two men on the outside could get in the middle and sleep.

As the miles dragged on men fell like flies from exhaustion and were shot. If a fellow soldier attempted to help one of his fallen companions, he would be killed. Artesian wells along the way were flowing with water, but if a man made a run for the water he was shot on the spot. John lost a hundred pounds during that march—down to sixty-five pounds—which he then weighed for the duration of his time as a POW.

When they arrived at San Fernando in Pangpanga, one hundred or more prisoners were packed at a time into WWI-era railroad boxcars to be taken to Camp O'Donnell. John was one of the first to be loaded so he was able to breathe by putting his nose up to a little crack in the side of the car. Many who were in the middle of the cars suffocated, and they would die standing up because there was no room to fall.

Conditions at Camp O'Donnell were even more unbearable than the march. Another 30,000 of the men died from starvation, disease, unsanitary conditions, injuries sustained in the march, and from the brutality of the Japanese guards at the camp. They were given one rice ball a day. There were only two water pipes in the camp and the water was only turned on once a day, so approximately one hundred men died daily.

The healthier men were put to work digging graves. Some of the very sick were buried alive, but those who refused to do the burying were shot. John said it was quite common to be talking to someone and have him just fall over dead in mid-sentence. John knew he had to get out of the camp to survive, so whenever the guards asked for volunteers for outside work, he would comply. But, with every passing day, his hatred for the Japanese grew stronger in John's heart.

On May 6, John was sent to Manila to help build

a bridge to replace one that the U.S. Marines had blown up during their retreat. The volunteers were stripped of all their clothing in the middle of town and made to swim back and forth across the river in the swift currents, pushing logs for the bridge as they swam. They wore armbands with a number, and were told that if anyone escaped the rest would be shot.

Eventually, one man came up missing and the guard was told to shoot ten prisoners—five on each side of the missing man's number. John was the sixth person and if any of the five had been sick that day, John would have moved into his spot. They were made to watch as the ten men were shot to death. John remembered with pain how one brother watched as his own twin was murdered.

After building other bridges and airstrips, John was transferred again, this time to Bilibid Prison in Manila. The next time he volunteered he was loaded onto a Japanese ship that the POWs called "Hell Ship." There, conditions were far worse than those on the death march and in the prison camps. On his particular ship, about 1,400 prisoners were crammed into the cargo area where they sat with their knees pulled tightly to their chests to make room for them all to fit. For thirty-nine days they sat this way without being able to move. The men who died were put overboard, while many of these ships were sunk by allied submarines because they were not marked as prison ships. John made it to Hong Kong, then to Formosa, and finally to Tokyo.

On January 26, 1945, John was moved to his final destination: Prison Camp Wakasen. Barefoot, and wearing only underwear, the men were forced to walk in hip-deep snow. Several of the men froze to death the first night. For seven months they worked in the lead and zinc mine as slave labor. One day a huge slab fell and pinned another man's legs. Six men picked it up and the others pulled him out. However, the next day when the six men tried to lift the slab, they couldn't budge it.

During this time John had another of his many miraculous interventions by God that once again saved his life. He was sent down four to five flights in the underground mine to a section where there were no signals or escape routes. The mine caved in that day and John began to tell God he didn't want to die—that if God would get him out, he would serve Him. Supernaturally, God showed John a ladder in this lower level that had not been there before, and they were able to make it to safety. When the guards insisted there was no way for them to have climbed out, John showed them the ladder. They quickly told him they didn't put it there and John said, "I know. Jesus did!"

God was doing miracles for John, but all the while the devil was contending for his life by filling him with more and more hatred. Once a Japanese guard stood him in a ditch filled with two feet of snow, then took a six-inch-by-six-inch timber and brutally struck him four times on his ear, rupturing the eardrum. There was so much hate in John by this time that he promised the man he would find him and kill him when the opportunity came. As soon as the war was declared over he took a pistol with three clips and ran down to look for the guard, but he was nowhere to be found. Instead of rejoicing that the war was over, all he could think about was retaliation. However, God had intervened again, keeping him from murdering this man.

After the second atomic bomb was dropped on

Nagasaki, Americans began dropping food from B-29 planes in fifty-five-gallon drums. Once he found a box of Snickers and ate all twenty-four in one sitting. That was probably another time when God saved his life. Eating that many Snickers at one time, after being starved for over three years, could easily have killed him. The war was finally over, but of the 75,000 soldiers who started the Death March from Bataan, only one in three survived to go home.

John married Carolyn Hardeman in February, 1947, and they had five children. Fifty years later, John felt a strong impression he was supposed to go back to Japan and help build a church, but hate still consumed his heart. It was on that first trip, after the YWAM leader kept delaying the first work day, that Carolyn finally had a dream in which she was told that John would not be allowed to build a church until he repented for the hatred he carried in his heart.

He couldn't bring himself to do that until God spoke to him and said, "You will either serve Me or you will serve the devil." That got John's attention and repentance began to come. John said, "Every time we went to Japan the hate was still there. But every time, little by little, it began to fade."

Then, on his last trip to Japan, he talked to an old man inside one of the churches he helped build and heard the apology for the wrong that had been done to him and to his other fellow Americans—an apology he had wanted so long to hear. At that point John finally began to ask forgiveness for the hatred in his heart.

From then on, whenever he saw a Japanese, he felt he was supposed to ask forgiveness for hating them all those years. Interestingly, it was an American Japanese man, George (Joe) Sakato, a Congressional

Medal of Honor recipient who fought for America in Europe, who presented John his Purple Heart. By then, after fifty years the hatred had been driven from his heart. Four times he and his wife have gone to Japan, staying ninety days on each trip and helping to build churches.

Author's interview with John Walker: "This is one of the most powerful testimonies I've heard on the transforming power of God to enable one to forgive his enemies. Since you went through years as a POW in World War II, you can speak from experience. What would you say to a military man who is struggling with unforgiveness because he is embittered by memories of the enemies he fought and the men he watched die?"

John replied, "You have to turn it over to the Lord, because if you don't, unforgiveness will eat you alive. You have to turn those memories over to the Lord, and then He will lead you and protect you."

The Miracle of Seadrift, Texas

Not One of Their Fifty-two Soldiers Died in the War

McCown Brothers

Author's Note: *One of my most memorable and exciting experiences came when I had the privilege of speaking to some of the residents of Seadrift, Texas, and hearing them tell stories of God's magnificent protection over their soldiers during WWII. This is their story of the boys who went off to war and the families who stayed behind to pray for their safety. Joe Fred Coward, along with Hollis and Gerald McCown, said that they experienced miraculous protection during World War II, and they knew why. A group of mothers and friends in their hometown of Seadrift, Texas, fervently prayed for their safety. Coward and the McCown brothers were among fifty-two soldiers whose photos were placed in a large picture frame at a church and prayed over daily until they returned. Everyone I interviewed was still excited to tell me, "All fifty-two came home!"*

World War II Prayer Board

It was the Psalm 91 promise of protection that the prayer warriors prayed over those young men, who were putting themselves in harm's way every day to protect their country. One of the intercessors said that

God had them literally bombard heaven. And one by one, every Seadrift soldier returned safely from the battlefields of Europe, the South Pacific, and the Far East, in spite of the fact that hundreds of thousands of American lives were lost on those battle fronts.

I spoke with Lora Weaver, who was one of those faithful intercessors. Even though she has enjoyed many years on this earth, and her hearing is not what it used to be, she still remembers with joy the abundance of faith they experienced in knowing that God was going to answer their prayers as they stood on the Ninety-first Psalm.

She said, "We read the passage every time we met. It promises that God gives his angels charge over us. God is awesome."

Mary Wilson Neill was another of the intercessors who said that some twenty women attended those prayer meetings every day. You can imagine the impression it made on the people in Seadrift when every one of the young men in their town came home from the war.

In particular, Fanny Maude (Granny) McCown was quite a prayer warrior. Known as a Five-Star Mother for having all five sons in WWII, she could often be heard crying out through tears as she prayed out loud in the Smoke House for the protection of her boys.

Scattered throughout the world, those young men blessed practically every branch of the Service. Glen McCown

was in the Army and fought in the Pacific Arena. Danger faced him every day of the war as he had the perilous job of going into caves throughout the islands, looking for Japanese. Eugene McCown served in the Navy in the South Pacific and was a constant target while operating landing crafts to lay down ground troops. Milton actively served in the Navy as well, throughout the war.

Another of Fanny McCown's sons, Gerald, joined the Air Force and fought in Europe. He was sent overseas in the largest convoy to ever cross the Atlantic Ocean, and they were forced to travel in total blackout at night, to go undetected by the enemy. The night before D-day he saw General Eisenhower talking to pilots and wishing them good luck. He pointed to Eisenhower and told his buddies, "Something big is going to be happening tomorrow. Wait, and see!"

That something big was the Normandy Invasion. Within less than twenty-four hours after seeing the general, he was flying over the English Channel. And he remembers, "I had never seen as many ships and planes in all my life—they literally covered the waters and the sky." Gerald also remembers vividly how a friend he met after arriving in Europe was fearful of what the next day would bring. Sure enough, the friend's plane was hit and the concussion from the explosion was so bad that it threw Gerald's plane up and dirt actually came through the cracks in the floorboard. What a difference it might have made if that young man had had a praying church back home.

During those perilous times Gerald McCown experienced the protective hand of God on numerous occasions. Some of his vivid memories came from the times when he helped drop supplies from an airplane to ground troops in England and France, as he stood on top of a thick steel plate because bullets came up through the bottom of the plane. Gerald said they would often fly behind enemy lines and drop supplies and food to General Patton and his ground troops, to help keep them moving as rapidly as possible across Europe to stop the Nazi advancement.

Hollis McCown, another of Fanny's sons, is still living to tell how he never left the States but knew his job of servicing the planes to keep them in optimum shape for our fliers—and refueling them for their important missions—was a vital contribution to the success of the war effort. Her sixth son entered WWII after the declaration was signed, then later fought again in the Korean War. What a heritage Fanny Maude McCown and her family have left for their descendants.

Joe Fred Coward, stationed in the Philippines, remembered barely escaping death when he drove an open army truck and felt something whiz by his head—so close that he said his hair turned up. Coward is still living and continues to thank God for the divine protection he knew he received on an almost daily basis. "I felt privileged to have been raised in a church that believed the Word and in the power of prayer," he said.

However, the incredible story of God's protection didn't end with WWII. Gerald's grandson, Sgt. Leslie King, served in Iraq. King has not only carried on the legacy of his grandfather and uncles, but the church in Seadrift has also continued in the famous heritage left to them.

He called his mother to say that something was not right. He didn't feel the shield of protection anymore for his men, and he knew something was badly amiss. At that time the family noticed all the military pictures were gone from the bulletin board. They had been taken down because the actual "war" was considered to be over.

Little did anyone know of the battles yet to be fought! After this was brought to the attention of the pastor, the photos were put back. Interestingly, without knowing that his picture had been removed and, subsequently, put back on display, Sgt. King wrote home again to say that his peace and security had returned. They didn't lose any more men and the troubles had begun to subside.

The family knew that it was no coincidence that the deaths and trouble occurred within the three-week period when the photos were out of sight. Even though the troops were being prayed for, there was something about corporate prayer from an entire church, having the pictures displayed, and having visual contact when they prayed, that made a big difference. What a powerful tool prayer is! (See Leslie King's testimony in his own words on page 235.)

Sergeant Harold Barclay
of Brownwood, Texas

Testimony by his daughter, Janie Boyd

Sergeant George Harold Barclay served in World War II in General Patton's 320th Infantry, U.S. Army, Company E. Continuous fear eliminated any expectation of ever returning to his wife and baby daughter. The same fear kept his wife terrified when she would see a Western Union truck delivering letters of war casualties.

Once a Western Union messenger came to her door by mistake and she said she froze with terror. Sometimes as many as six weeks would go by without a letter, during which time the media reported that half of Barclay's company had been killed. The Battle of the Bulge saw his whole outfit cut off from the rest of the army.

Finally, however, a letter came from Harold saying that God had given him Psalm 91, and he now had absolute certainty that he would come home without even an injury. So certain was he of this promise in Psalm 91 that, when the medics said they needed volunteers to go to the front lines to bring back the injured, Harold volunteered and made repeated trips under extreme enemy fire, saving many lives.

The citation for the Bronze Star Award he received said "for bravery," but Harold insisted that it wasn't bravery since he knew nothing would happen to him because of the covenant promise God had given to him in Psalm 91. When he came home without a scratch, it was obvious that angels had indeed borne him up in their hands, allowing no evil to befall him (Psalm 91:11–12).

Don Beason, Navy
2nd Class Yeoman

When I read *Psalm 91: God's Umbrella of Protection,* it answered so many questions I had about divine protection during my life. I was saved when I was young and thought I would go to heaven when I died, but I was led to believe that I would probably suffer through life like the rest of the world does—with sickness and accidents. I wondered why that had to be. Thank God I had a praying mother!

Now I am seventy-nine years old, but I feel about thirty. I have never had a broken bone or an operation. In fact, I have not been in a hospital in sixty years. Likewise, I've not been to a medical doctor in the last fifteen or twenty years, and I do not take any medicine or nutritional supplements. I give all the credit to God's Word.

I was raised in the sand hills of Nebraska, around horses and cattle, where accidents, injuries, and even death occurred on a regular basis. While growing up we rode and tried to break every kind of animal we could get a rope or saddle on. I have seen many others injured around me, but I never was. I wondered why. I thank God for a praying, believing mother!

I enlisted in the Navy during World War II, so I could see the world and have a girl in every port. I never got out of the United States, but I did get into the wine, women, and song. I saw other men come back to the base with injuries, sickness, or sexually transmitted diseases, but nothing like that ever happened to me. I wondered why. I thank God for a praying, believing mother and a forgiving heavenly Father!

I boxed in high school and in the Navy, but never had any of the typical injuries along the way. After I got out of the Navy I had a few back alley or street fights, and two of them were so bad I could have been badly hurt. One time I ran into two men in a bar, one of whom pulled a knife on me. I beat them so badly one ended up in the hospital, but I never even had a black eye or a bloody nose.

The next serious fight came in the wee hours of the night after a dance, where ten or fifteen cowboys stood in the street drinking beer and talking about their times in the service. When I told them about just getting out of the Navy, one of them called me a liar because I looked so young for my age. I knocked him down and it looked like all the rest were going to beat me up, so I asked them if they were men enough to do it one at a time instead of all at once. They thought they could do it that way, but after I whipped three of them no one else wanted to fight. Again, I never even had a black eye or bloody nose—or even a scratch.

Once more I also wondered why I never got hurt! It could not have been because I was so big and tough, because I was only 5'10" and weighed 150 pounds. *I thank God for my mother's prayers when I was not putting Christ first in my life.*

When I got into the insurance business I was driving about sixty thousand miles a year, coming home late at night. After an evening appointment I would sometimes doze off, but something would wake me up every time before I would run off the road or cross the middle line. That was more than forty years ago, and I have never run off the road or had an accident. Back then I thought it had to be more than luck, but I was not sure.

About twenty years ago I got into the Word and found out who I was in Christ, and who Christ was in me, and that I had been given dominion over all the works of the enemy. Satan has tried but he has not been able to put anything on me and never will.

When I read *Psalm 91: God's Umbrella of Protection* it revealed the supernatural protection I have had in more detail. I saw that we have, as Christians, a supernatural, protection covenant. It does not matter whether we are young or old, whether we are in the service during wartime or facing the struggles and battles we go through in everyday life. We do not have to wait until we get to heaven to enjoy the supernatural, exceedingly abundant, more than you can ask for or think about, good life that God has for us right here on earth.

It is such a desire of my heart to get this message out to other Christians that I am buying these *Psalm 91: God's Umbrella of Protection* books by the case and distributing them to churches and people I meet on the street. This is a message that needs to be heard. What a difference it would make if fathers and mothers would just teach their children to believe, and to confess every day that they have lifelong protection through the Word.

Jesus came to restore what was lost in the Garden of Eden. And according to the Word it is available to us today if we really believe without doubting. What a blessing to be able to enter into the peace and rest without all the fear and worry that is in the world. It works for me and it will work for you.

Actor Jimmy Stewart, Air Force, Combat Pilot and Bombardier Trainer

It is not surprising that James Stewart felt a call to serve his country during WWII. He came from a very patriotic family with a military history. Both of his grandfathers served in the Civil War, and his father fought in the Spanish-American War and WWI.

Jimmy Stewart learned to fly and received his private pilot's license in 1935. He enlisted in the Army on March 22, 1941. Though he desired to fly as a combat pilot, he was at first used mostly for publicity. At his own expense he took additional flight training so he could qualify for combat. He received his commission after the attack on Pearl Harbor.

Early in the war, Jimmy Stewart served as a Bombardier trainer. He was eventually qualified on B-17s and was attached as Operations Officer with the 445th Bomb Group, 703rd squadron. Within a month he was put in command of the squadron. From 1944 to 1945 he served as chief of staff, 2nd Combat Wing, 2nd Division, 8th Air Force.

Throughout the war he carried with him a copy of the 91st Psalm, a gift from his father. When Stewart enlisted in the Army Air Corps and prepared to go overseas, his father was overcome with emotion. He choked up when he tried to bid his son farewell, so he wrote a note for Jimmy to read later. After being shipped out, Jimmy read what his father had been unable to say out loud. The note read:

My dear Jim-Boy,
Soon after you read this letter, you will be on
your way to the worst sort of danger. Jim, I
am banking on the enclosed copy of the 91st
Psalm. The thing that takes the place of fear
and worry is the promise of these words. I am
staking my faith in these words. I feel sure
that God will lead you through this mad
experience. I can say no more. I only continue
to pray.
Goodbye, my dear. God continue to bless and
keep you. I love you more than I can tell you.
Dad

Jimmy Stewart held Psalm 91 dear to his heart, saying, "What a promise for an airman. I placed in His hands the squadron I would be leading. And, as the psalmist promised, I felt myself borne up."[10]

His family's prayers for his safe return were answered. After twenty combat missions, Jimmy Stewart returned home, a decorated hero and unharmed. During the height of the battle Stewart said he learned to lean on the words of his tattered copy of Psalm 91.

Nazi Prison Camp

by Corrie ten Boom[11]

Many people came to know and trust the Lord during World War II. One was an Englishman who was held in a German prison camp for a long period of time. One day he read Psalm 91. "Father in heaven," he prayed, "I see all these men dying around me, one after the other. Will I also have to die here? I am still young and I very much want to work in Your kingdom here on earth." He received this answer: "Rely on what you have just read and go home!" Trusting in the Lord, he got up and walked into the corridor toward the gate. A guard called out, "Prisoner, where are you going?"

"I am under the protection of the Most High," he replied. The guard came to attention and let him pass, for Adolf Hitler was known as "the most high."

He came to the gate, where a group of guards stood. They commanded him to stop and asked where he was going. "I am under the protection of the Most High." All the guards stood at attention as he walked out the gate.

The English officer made his way through the German countryside and eventually reached England, where he told how he had made his escape. He was the *only one* to come out of that prison alive.

Gene Porter 1924–2002
WWII, Staff Sergeant Infantry

Bernice McCuistion met Gene Porter at Howard Payne University in Brownwood, Texas. They fell in love, but out of respect for their parents' wishes they did not marry until matters were more settled concerning the draft situation in the early days of World War II.

College students stood on standby as the world went to war, but sure enough, Gene Porter was drafted, received his orders and was shipped out. On his person he carried a *Gideon New Testament Bible and the Psalms*, with his girlfriend's picture tucked inside. He would read Psalm 91 and quote it over and over, because he believed *prayer changes things*. He said it was his means of surviving.

He entered the war in Southern France in Marseilles, where there was heavy battle. He literally walked across Europe, fighting as he went—through France and on into Germany. When the war ended he had walked and fought all the way into Austria.

It has been said many times, "There are no atheists in a foxhole," and many made commitments to the Lord when they saw death face-to-face. When they see war, most men become either bitter or better, and Gene Porter became more grounded in his faith.

All his letters to Bernice were censored by the United States Government to remove any information about troop movements, but they did reveal heavy combat situations, describing a war far worse than anyone could imagine. A shell burst close to him, stunned him, and knocked him into an embankment. He knew God had spared him. He was given the assignment to go behind enemy lines to get some telephone equipment, but when he returned, his company had pulled back and he was surrounded by the enemy. He knew it was only God's grace that enabled him to escape and rejoin his company.

Another strategic battle occurred when American troops in Mulhaus railhead captured this major rail center from the Germans. However, after they gave it to the French to secure, the French lost it. The Americans were then given the assignment to take it back. Letters slowed down and neither Bernice nor his mother received word from him for six weeks. Many prayers went up on his behalf. But he escaped without injury and returned home to a hero's welcome. He married Bernice, his college sweetheart, and settled into fifty-eight years of a happy marriage.

Gene would watch World War II movies but made very few comments on what he had seen. However, in one especially candid moment, he told his wife that even the most graphic movies like *Saving Private Ryan* did not adequately describe the horrors he had seen as a young soldier. He said even the most realistic and explicit of Hollywood movies glamorize war, and there was no glamour to it, only horrors.

She asked him how often he thought about the war and he replied, "Not a day goes by that I don't think about it!" Gene Porter was thoroughly convinced that God brought him home and that the pocket Bible with Psalm 91 surely did have promises which protect a man in the worst of conditions.

He was the only man in his company who was not wounded or killed.

Jefferson Bass Adams
1st Sergeant, WWII
36th Division, Army

Tribute: A Family Love Story

Author's Note: *Given so many challenges to military marriages, I am especially gratified to include this tribute to JB and Francis Adams, parents of my good friend, Kay Sheffield, and grandparents to our precious daughter-in-law, Sloan. This love story is an inspiration for all times, and a family treasure.*

When JB and his two buddies Allen and Skinny were drafted into the service during WWII, they were sent to Florida for training. It was hard for these young men to leave their wives, knowing they would be separated for at least two years.

However, those spunky eighteen-year-old wives had other plans. With one suitcase apiece, in a thirties Plymouth that was barely travel-worthy, they set out from Texas to follow their husbands. Once, when the car ran out of water, the resourceful threesome pulled off a hubcap, climbed a fence, brought back hubcaps full of water from a pond, and filled the radiator. In spite of head gasket problems in Mississippi and flat tires in the rain, nothing could stop them. They followed their guys through Florida, North and South Carolina, Virginia, and on into Massachusetts, locating the army bases and renting rooms in local boarding houses.

Each time the guys were transferred, the girls

were made to promise they would go immediately back home to Texas. However, no sooner would the guys find themselves at their new base than the girls would show up. Once, when the company was doing maneuvers at a new base, the guys looked up just in time to see the faithful old Plymouth come rolling by. Late that night when JB got off duty at 2 A.M. and located the boarding house where he was told the girls would be, he opened the door to find stairs and several closed doors at the top of the stairs. Just as he was pondering where Francis might be, a hand suddenly came out of one of the doors and simply pointed to a room where he found Francis waiting for him with what only a woman could bring in one suitcase. She was a "nester." In that one suitcase she brought only two dresses in order to leave room for the tablecloth, curtains, two plates, and a flower vase to make each place a "home away from home."

When finances got low, the girls simply found jobs. At one of their temporary homes they discovered that the huge bump in the road in front of their boarding house caused produce to bounce off the local farm truck every afternoon as it passed. The girls would sit on the porch, waiting to see what would fall. That would be their dinner. Like gypsies, they moved all over the U.S. throughout the men's training for overseas duty.

After being sent initially to Africa, JB was among the first American troops to hit the continent of Europe at the Salerno Invasion in Italy. The war was fierce, but God was faithful to His promises. JB recalled three instances when God's protection was miraculous.

First, JB's company was ready to cross the Rapido River that surrounded Monte Cassino, where the

Germans were using the monastery on top of that mountain as an outpost. Three separate times the orders changed just five minutes before JB was to cross. Of the men who were sent across, 90 percent were killed—more than two thousand men. Second, another miraculous protection came when JB and a buddy were filling their canteens at a creek, and a bullet whizzed between them. Third, when his company was ready to move forward at Mount Lungo, a herd of goats came out of nowhere, detonating the mines in the field they were about to cross. Not one man was killed crossing that field.

Colonel Jim Ammerman

Jim Ammerman lived during the Depression, when times were really hard. His dad's decision to withdraw their savings from the bank to help with family needs came to nothing when he found that the trustees had taken the money and burned the bank so there would be no records. That blow was followed by losing all of their worldly possessions when the house they were renting burned down.

When most young men would have turned bitter and angry, Jim instead was driven to seeking God more fervently than ever before. Because of a terrible drought that destroyed the crops in 1938, it gave Jim time to read the Bible through in a ninety-day period. He had asked Jesus to be Savior of his life at age nine, but now, at thirteen, Jim prayed that God would take complete charge of his life.

Immediately, during one eventful all-night prayer session by himself, three life-changing things happened. First, he was filled with the Holy Spirit (as a Baptist boy he didn't know what to call it at the time). Second, a lifetime of hearing God's voice began, the first example of which was an utterance instructing him to keep his life pure, to keep himself for the one girl that God had prepared to be his wife, and to refuse to smoke or drink alcohol. Last but not least, he discovered the next morning that he had been healed from a speech impediment that had plagued his entire childhood. For the first time in his life he was able to speak without a lisp. After that, a dedication to studying his Bible became his passion.

God has been faithful through the years to give Colonel Ammerman a supernatural word of knowledge from time to time, to guide his decisions and keep his life on target for God. Once, while praying in the woods, a word of knowledge told him, "I will use you to teach Army officers about Me." He didn't realize that word was going to take a great number of years before it came to pass—and ironically, Jim joined the Navy first!

However, just as Jim, barely seventeen, was getting ready to leave for the Naval Training Academy after the attack on Pearl Harbor, a pretty, fourteen-year-old blond girl named Charlene caught his attention as she took part in the Sunday school opening exercises. That meeting was certainly destined to play a big part in Jim's future.

From naval training he served on a destroyer, the USS *John Erickson*, making six trips across the Atlantic and taking him into the war in North Africa and the invasion of Sicily. He was prepared to put in for Navy Flight School, become a Navy aviator, and have a bright future in the Navy as an officer, but the realization that God was calling him into the ministry changed all that.

He was wrestling with God when his ship ran into a wolf pack of German submarines. He was thrown from his bunk as his ship suffered extensive damage from two ships colliding because of a missed signal, but God delivered him out of trouble.

His fear that Charlene (the girl back home) might not be pleased with his decision to go into the ministry was unfounded. Since God always confirms His word, Charlene knew and approved before Jim ever had a chance to tell her himself. During one of his leaves he persuaded Charlene to get married, and proudly reported to pilot's training as a married man. After almost two years of flight training, the men in that squadron were tested in pressure chambers for human body responses and reactions for high altitude flight above 40,000 feet until their bodies could no longer handle it. Jim and the few who completed the test program were told that they were qualified to begin flying in all jet airplanes. These would be the first two jet squadrons in the U.S. Navy at the close of World War II. However, in spite of this tremendous opportunity to be a part of this elite group, Jim chose to leave the Navy to follow the call on his life to be a pastor.

Private pastoral ministry also had its excitement. At his first pastorate at Grove Springs in southern Missouri, Jim found a man sleeping in his car in the church parking lot. After inviting him to come inside for the service, Jim found that the man was William Brannon, the evangelist whom God was using mightily at that time in a healing ministry.

After preaching the morning service, Brannon went on his way. That night, however, after Jim gave an altar call for salvation in his Baptist church, three sensational miracles happened. One lady, who had previously had a heart attack and was thought to be dead, went down in the power of the Spirit. Jim had never seen anything like it and thought she had another heart attack, but instead, she was miraculously healed and never had another problem with her heart.

Another lady who was going blind had her eyes

restored that night and was still pursuing her painting career many years later. And a most sensational miracle occurred when a man who had not been seen in public for twelve years, because of a disease that made his face and the skin on his body lumpy and scaly, resembling that of lizard, was completely healed over the next few days and restored to society. Attendance increased immediately, and many were saved.

When the Korean War began, his Navy chaplain from flight school gave Jim a call to reenlist. Jim wasn't sure he wanted to go back into the service, but God gave him a spiritual dream in which he saw himself dressed in an Army uniform with a parachute and standing with Army paratroopers. In the dream they were getting on a very different-looking plane that had twin booms instead of a fuselage that went back to the tail of the plane. He made his jump and when he touched the ground the dream ended.

Interestingly, when he finished Airborne school as a paratrooper chaplain and was preparing to make his first jump, the airplane he was scheduled to board was the same plane he had seen in the dream. When he made his jump it was so much like the dream he had of jumping that Jim said, "My first jump was actually my second jump."

Since he wanted to be a chaplain to guys who were not walking with God at all, when the Chief of Chaplains Office in Washington DC called to ask if he would consider volunteering to take the Green Beret Special Forces Training, Jim considered it a privilege. They transported him to Bad Tolz, Germany. This had been the place where Hitler's SS Officers were trained, so Jim began claiming this territory for God in his prayer time. It wasn't long before the services he conducted—two in the morning and one at night—couldn't accommodate all the people who were coming.

Jim was already a military paratrooper, a *Master Blaster* as they called them, but he joined the Trojans, a sports parachute club. He had made a hundred jumps but no free falls. Since he was a novice, he would read books on the subject and talk to the experts. Needless to say, Jim's jumping from airplanes was not Charlene's favorite thing to have him do, especially when he told of the spins one could experience when jumping and how, if they got "red eye" they were dead. The instructor had a slogan: "Red is dead."

Once, during an air show when thirteen hundred parachutes filled the skies over Germany, Jim's four children noticed that one of the men fell into the open chute of the parachute below him. After slipping and sliding from one parachute to the next (actually jumping on three chutes), he finally got in the clear and opened his chute, just in time, seconds before impact. Later at the dinner table, when the children very excitedly ask who the man was doing the spectacular maneuvers, Jim sheepishly admitted that he was the man.

During their night jumps, they had to time the opening of their chutes with a stopwatch since they couldn't see the ground and the chutes didn't open automatically. That period in Jim's life was very fruitful, producing many incredible stories of men that he led to the Lord—men who had felt that their lives were beyond God's help.

When asked if Jim had any Psalm 91 protection testimonies, his answer was, "Many." For example, when two prison escapees had Jim at gunpoint and realized that their first plan had failed, they decided to kill him and go to Plan B. They had nothing to lose—they had already been convicted of murder. But Jim, confident of God's protection, was able to convince them to turn themselves in. Not only was it a miraculous escape for Jim, but he also made it in time to preach at the second church service that morning.

Another time when God's Psalm 91 protection was obvious occurred when he went with a fellow chaplain on a call. After ringing the doorbell and being told to come in, a butcher knife sailed past his head and stuck in the wall as he walked through the door. The woman had mistaken him for her husband!

They also saw their Psalm 91 covenant working to protect their children. For example, when European doctors gave up on their son, Steve, in 1961, after he received a serious concussion, God took over and restored him to health—much to the surprise of the doctors. The next morning when they found Steve fully recovered, he told them about a man dressed in white who had sat by his bedside all night.

Again in 1961, when Beth, their daughter, received a serious head injury in a car wreck on the autobahn, Jim received a call that said, "If you want to see your daughter alive, get to the emergency room quick!"

Other channels had planned to notify him that his daughter had been killed in a serious wreck because her brain waves were flat. Jim said that all he could do was stand there weeping, not even having the faith to ask if God could restore his fourteen-year-old daughter.

Charlene just kept wiping the blood off her daughter's lifeless body until Jim finally took her home, but before the night was over they received a call that their daughter was alive! God miraculously restored Beth to health.

When their infant son, Mark, started having regular seizures following a serious car wreck, the doctors wanted to cut away part of his skull in the hope that it might help. Jim and Charlene decided against that procedure and continued to trust God for healing. Finally, God used a chiropractor to correct the problem. In total, the devil tried to steal three of their four children but God's power protected every one of them and restored them all completely.

One time when Jim was praying, a heavenly form became visible in the sky and he heard these words come forth: "The most difficult, trying time of your life is just ahead, but do not fear. I will be with you." His career was going good; he was already a major and due for a promotion; and his family was all well.

Shortly thereafter, however, as the Vietnam War began heating up, Jim was assigned to the 3rd Special Forces Group. He had to meet with different commanders, and one of those commanders asked him to do some spying for him at headquarters. Jim refused and the disgruntled commander said, "You will be sorry!"

The man made good his threat by having him falsely accused by some chaplains who were angry with Jim for not overlooking their ungodly behavior. They lied under oath, swearing to things that were not true, and got him fired. He remembered the word that the Lord told him. He was locked up and the nightmare went on for five months before he was released. Because of the allegations, he was told that he would never be eligible for promotion, but

God protected his reputation by having an official record changed—something no one had ever before heard of happening. Instead of losing all chances of advancement, Jim spent a year in Vietnam, three years in Fort Hood and was later sent to Germany where he served as Fifth Corps chaplain as a full colonel with eighty-three chaplains under his command. God does have a way of vindicating His own.

He finally retired after a rich three years as chaplain for the post and the Command and General Staff College at Ft. Leavenworth, Kansas. Jim and Charlene spent the first year of retirement traveling the entire world, sightseeing and visiting missionaries.

Now that Colonel Ammerman has retired from the U.S. Army, he is continuing to influence history. He has started a seminary to train evangelistic chaplains in Caracas, Venezuela, which is now fully accredited. With each undertaking God has led him into, in spite of opposition from many people, it has been God who brought it to pass.

Once, when the government agent from Venezuela emphatically told him, "No!" he knew he was engaged in spiritual warfare. Knowing that only God could change the situation, he excused himself and left the office, walked behind a large plant in the lobby and cried out earnestly for God to intervene.

When he walked back into the office the entire atmosphere had changed and the agent gave his permission. Colonel Ammerman also heads up the Chaplaincy of Full Gospel Churches, with headquarters in Dallas, Texas. This organization is responsible for influencing legislation on a national level. We can thank this organization for tremendous strides in keeping us from losing some of our Christian rights in our armed forces.

This man, who has walked with God from his youth to the present time, has seen supernatural Psalm 91 protection during a remarkable time in history and is a role model and a hero in an age when good role models and true heroes are hard to find.

Author's Note: Jim's story is told in Supernatural Events in the Life of an Ordinary Man, *by Chaplain Jim Ammerman. ISBN: 1-883893-48-8.*

Chester William Egert
WWII Army Chaplain

His son, First Lt Philip Egert, U.S. Army, Korea
Grandson, LTC Chaplain Chester C. Egert, Iraq

These three Egerts were ordinary men who went to war because their country asked them to go. They were peace loving men, but they were willing to lay their lives down in a foreign country to help preserve freedom and democracy where there was a threat from the enemy.

1st Lt Philip Egert in Korea

On August 11, 1950, Philip Dornon Egert, just out of officer candidate school, was put on a ship to Korea with both young graduates and veteran soldiers. Philip would quip that the young soldiers were so green behind the ears that many of them didn't even know where Korea was on the map. Typical of how the next eighteen months was going to be, Egert was almost killed within hours of their landing. It was a rude awakening for this forward observer and the two lieutenants who were with him as they barely escaped with their lives.

This terrible firefight, which immediately introduced him to Korea as soon as he left the ship, gave him a baptism by fire that never stopped until he came home in January 1952. But throughout his time in Korea and for the rest of his life, he claimed that the God of Psalm 91:7 never failed him once: "A thousand shall fall at thy side, and ten thousand at thy right hand; but it shall not come nigh thee."

Young soldiers who had never seen combat were thrown into hand-to-hand warfare—harsh, high-casualty, life-taking combat. These youth were not prepared for the North Koreans, and he said he saw only one chaplain in his entire deployment. And that happened when he specifically sought him out at a memorial service. Young men who had grown up in a home where they had only known love and compassion found themselves thrust in a loveless, bloody war. They were helping bring freedom to a country they had never even known existed.

But through it all, Psalm 91 was Egert's mainstay. In fact, he wrote that he would not be alive if it were not for the promises of protection in that psalm. Even though he couldn't read directly from it because of the constant heat of battle, he carried the little *Gideon New Testament with the Psalms* in his pocket throughout the entire war, and over and over he clung to the memorized words in the ninety-first chapter. With thousands dying all around him, Egert said that he quoted verse 7 with every fiber of his being for the next year and a half.

For several months after his return, Egert was tormented by nightmares. He couldn't talk about the war, but at night his vivid subconscious memories would return frequently and he would relive his hand-to-hand combat in dreams. God delivered him from these nightmares within a few months through prayer, but it was decades before he decided to tell about his experiences in the war. In 1987, Egert recorded his memories for his sons and grandchildren. Here are some of those miracle deliverances in his own words.

A Psalm 91 intervention: Navy arrives in the nick of time

The North Koreans had some Russian tanks sitting at the foot of the mountain on the north side, and they were just really pounding us. Remember, we didn't have air strikes back then. Close support of the troops was a new thing. Jets were very rare. Most of the planes that did fly for close support were propeller-driven Navy planes, and we had a hard time that night.

There were three or four tanks that were giving our infantry fits, and we were extremely short on artillery. I could see the tanks firing from the top of the mountain there, and I called in a fire mission. They said, "I am sorry, we have no ammunition." God intervened in an impossible situation. Just as our situation looked hopeless, I heard someone say, "Prepare to observe Willie Peter." William Peter, or White Phosphorus, is a dreaded explosive substance that could not be extinguished by water or any counteracting chemical. Once on an individual, it would burn through clothing, skin or almost any other material until it burned itself out. Then, just in the nick of time, out of nowhere God had a naval battleship sitting off the coast, and he turned his big guns on them, and took over the fire mission from the coordinates that I had given them. The Navy did a fantastic job of destroying the enemy.

We pulled out of Sobuksan and went from one village to the next, pushing the North Koreans back, having firefights day after day. We would advance as one battalion, and one battalion of artillery would advance. It was sort of a hop, skip, and jump type of advancement in support of the units, but we kept moving.

Because we were short of artillery and infantry officers, sometimes I, a twenty-one-year-old whippersnapper, even led some infantry patrols. We pushed forward; I got another sergeant to be my radio man, and we pushed out of the Pusan Perimeter and finally up to Seoul.

Of course, the North Koreans had really dug in around Seoul, and so we had a real battle there. About that time, as we were pushing up, General Douglas MacArthur was planning the Inchon Invasion. So we caught the Koreans in a Pincer effect, and we really devastated the North Koreans with that Pincers Movement. MacArthur was a brilliant tactician (understatement), and had it not been for God using him I really don't think I would be here now.

Anyway, we devastated the North Korean Army and pushed on up past the 38th Parallel. By this time it was getting pretty cold in Korea, and we had no winter clothing. We saw Thanksgiving come in 1950, and we saw Thanksgiving go! The only thing we got for our turkey dinner was another can of C-Rations. So we pushed on and pushed on, and in fact, I was one of the Forward Observers who fired artillery on Pyongyang, the capital of North Korea, and we pushed on up until we literally got to the Yalu River of North Korea, which separates North Korea and China.

By this time we had liberated all of North Korea and we could have stopped the Chinese, if President Truman had allowed MacArthur to do it. But we were given orders to the effect that we could not fire on them, even though we could see the Chinese across the river forming masses of troops. Our planes could not strafe them or bomb them, and therefore the Chinese and the remnants of the North Korean Army counterattacked and came back at us, hitting us really hard. But God was faithful to bring me home.

Over and over through those years, Egert saw the promises in Psalm 91 fulfilled. And, when Egert's wife, Ruth, later asked him, "What allowed you to come back home alive?" he said, "God's providence. I should have died many times. But Psalm 91:7 kept me alive."

The words burned into his heart, allowing him to cling to them daily in battle, much of which was the most intense kind of combat. When Egert returned home in 1952, he was promoted to a first lieutenant. Egert expressed it beautifully when he stated, "I'm proud to be an American veteran who served twenty-four years for this country, and may God bless this country as we continue to honor Him."

Philip Egert followed in the footsteps of his father, Chester William Egert, a World War II army chaplain who participated in the Normandy Invasion. It was Philip's father who taught him to stand on God's Word to get through the battles. At the Normandy beachhead, Chester W. Egert learned the value of the Word of God. When it was his unit's turn to launch onto the beaches they were held up by the many wounded who were being brought back from the front lines. In later years he said, "The blood was so thick they were mopping it up like running water on the floor."

In spite of the horrible conditions, Chester refused to leave those transports until he had prayed over every single one of the men who returned. Many stories testify of the divine protection he received when his life was spared in battle after battle, and especially as he went into the thick of battle behind the first wave of men on the shores of Normandy.

Chaplain (Lt. Col.) Chester C Egert followed in the footsteps of his grandfather and his father. In 2003 he deployed to Iraq as the Division Chaplain for the 101st Airborne Division based at Fort Campbell, Kentucky. Just as the promises in Psalm 91 protected his father and grandfather, he too experienced that divine protection. There were close calls and narrow escapes for Chester, but one in particular stands out.

When his wife heard the news of two Blackhawks that crashed in Mosul, she had not heard from him on the day of the crashes. As families at Fort Campbell awaited word on the fate of their spouses, the community turned into a ghost town. Chester had been scheduled to fly that particular day in November 2003, but she didn't know whether he was on one of the two ill-fated flights.

Meanwhile, Chester's mother, Ruth, had not heard from her son for several days. Watching the world news on television about the crashing of the helicopters, she wondered, like Rhoda, if Chester was on one of those flights. Not knowing the answer, she turned to God in prayer and asked God directly, "Is my son dead or alive?"

In the midst of the turmoil, she opened her Bible and with tears in her eyes as she looked at the pages, suddenly the verse literally rose off the page. Her eyes fell on the words from 2 Samuel 14:11, "'As surely as the Lord lives,'" He said, 'Not one hair of your son's head will fall to the ground'" (NIV).

God had spoken! Her son was alive, and no matter what he was experiencing in Iraq—even if he had crashed—she knew everything was going to turn out for his good because of the verse that God had supernaturally given her in prayer. God had spoken through His Word.

When Ruth learned of Chester's safety, she kept praying for the families of the troops who gave their lives that day in Iraq. There were five soldiers who survived from one of the helicopters. Seventeen soldiers and crew members died between the two Blackhawks. Psalm 91 is more meaningful every day. Chaplain Chester C. Egert now makes the third generation of Egerts who have trusted the Lord in war.

Author's Note: *Chester C. Egert was promoted to Colonel on August 31, 2006.*

Abel F. Ortega, Corporal
World War II Survivor of
Bataan Death March
Korean War

By John Johnson (grandson)

My grandfather, Abel Ortega, shared the wonderful testimony of how he survived the brutality of the torture inflicted by his Japanese captors during World War II. Although he had not yet surrendered his life to Christ he came from a Christian home in which his family did not begin a meal until each child in the family quoted a Bible verse. His father was a Methodist minister and his mother was a strong believer in Jesus Christ.

My grandfather later realized that the prayers of his faithful family members had protected him under some of the most dangerous conditions, such as the Bataan Death March when they were made to walk for over ninety miles with little to no food or water. He watched as his fellow soldiers were bayoneted, shot, burned, decapitated, and left for dead on the side of the road. As a result of the prayers of his mother, God provided him strength and opportunities to survive in situations that killed many of his fellow soldiers.

When these American troops were bombed in the Philippines they were only just making preparations for war. They had few to no weapons and very little food left. The bombing of the ships in Pearl Harbor had cut off the food supply. For five months the American troops fought as they lived off whatever they could find on the island. They ate the water buffalo and the cavalry horses, and since they were

172

fighting in the jungle they actually lived off the snakes they killed—in fact, anything that moved, they killed and ate. After five months the men were so weak they were forced to surrender, but they had no idea of the cruelty that awaited them.

The Bataan Death March claimed the lives of thousands of the troops, but even after getting to the first POW camp an estimated one hundred prisoners died daily. There was scarcely any food at all and two water faucets in the entire camp which only dripped water for a few hours a day before it was cut off entirely. Men lined up with their canteens, only to die standing in the water line.

Abel was among the stronger who would bury the dead. After a rain they would drag the decaying bodies (the stench was almost unbearable) away from the camp, dig shallow graves with their hands, and then pack mud over them to cover them up. Each grave had a stick cross with the soldier's dog tags hung over the cross.

Although the Japanese murdered many American prisoners, they also exploited them as slave labor to accomplish tasks they could not complete on their own. These slaves were forced to work long hours each day, under horrible conditions, with absolutely no breaks and just enough water to keep them alive. The food was a bowl of water in which the green tops off the carrots had been boiled with a little rice. They were forced to build airfields, rebuild bridges, and drain lakes so more rice could be planted. The prisoners were cruelly beaten if they failed to obey the foreign commands, and since English was not spoken, they were forced to learn Japanese.

At one point in the war the Japanese military

jammed small ships full of thousands of prisoners in order to prevent them from being liberated when allied troops closed in on their location. While the prisoners were being loaded into the ships, referred to as *Hell ships* due to the horrible conditions, the Lord answered the prayers of a faithful mother by protecting my grandfather with divine favor.

As he was boarding his particular *Hell* ship, Abel saw a small homemade tin can, and an audible voice said, "Pick it up." That "can" literally saved his life. The men were taken eighteen feet down into the lower level of the ship, and more than five hundred prisoners were forced to live for over a month in a forty-five-square-foor area where they could barely move. But Abel found himself under a small hole in the ceiling and was able to utilize his can to collect fresh rainwater that dripped into the ship, to use for drinking and trading. It was a divine provision. He was the only one who had any kind of container.

While many died of thirst on that voyage, that tin can saved his life and he knew it was because he had a family praying for him. They were on the first ship for thirty-eight days, and Abel said Americans were not used to being so crowded and mistreated. As a result, many of the guys went crazy and died. Also, because the ships were not marked as POW vessels, many of the 1800 men in those POW liners were killed by bombs from American planes.

My grandfather was known as the camp artist. When the war ended and the Japanese guards fled, he became the Betsy Ross of the POW camp. The men in that camp will never forget that he was the one who went to the prisoners from the different countries (e.g., the United States, England, Holland, Australia), drew their descriptions of their flags, took the different colored silk parachutes to a tailor in the nearby town, and had him make the national flag of each country represented. He even gathered up some food to pay the tailor for his work.

Dressed in the dirty, worn-out uniforms that they found, they then tied those flags on long bamboo poles and had a flag-raising ceremony. Some of the men found instruments in the village and formed a band to play the national anthems.

Abel said, "There are no words to describe the feelings that surged through our beings, standing there in those dirty uniforms and watching the flag of our country being raised, listening to our little band play our national anthem as we sang the words so passionately, with all of our gusto and knowing we were indeed free—even in that enemy country."

Shortly afterward my grandfather was joyfully reunited with his mother. Later he married and began to obey the command to be fruitful and multiply.

Then, in 1950, he was drafted to return to war in Korea. This caused him some inner turmoil, since he had witnessed firsthand the death and destruction of war, and he realized that he now had the responsibility and spiritual authority over a wife and children. Previously, as a young, single man he had the protective cover of his faithful mother and father. But the reality of having to face war again, this time with his own family at home, led him to the realization that he had to surrender his life to Christ in order to make it through. He did this very thing prior to leaving home to serve his country once again, in the 3rd Division 15th Infantry Regiment, Company G, in overseas combat.

As a new Christian my grandfather was faced with another challenge. He was obedient to fulfill his service to his country, but the love of God in his heart made him hesitate at the thought of having to kill his enemies. Soon after praying to God for guidance in this troubling matter, he led his unit during an advance on a Korean hillside. Noticing the movement of a possible enemy nearby, and following his military training, he raised his rifle and attempted to fire. However, the gun failed to function when he pulled the trigger. Believing this to be confirmation that God had answered his prayer by showing him he would not have to kill the enemy, he made a decision that day to remove the bullet clip out of his gun for the remainder of his time at war. God supernaturally protected him and gave him the desire of his heart. He did not have to kill anyone. He literally ran through bullets without anything striking him.

God is so good! My grandfather's blessings did not stop there. Due to his bilingual ability he was placed in charge of a group of minority soldiers for the remainder of the war. He prayed for his troops regularly and the Lord faithfully answered the prayers. Not only did my grandfather safely return home to his family, but he did not lose one soldier in his charge during all his operations in the Korean War. This is an amazing testimony of God's awesome Psalm 91 covenant of protection.

Author's Note: *Mr. Ortega received twenty medals and citations: three Presidential Unit Citations, including the Republic of Philippines Presidential Unit Citation and the Republic of Korean Presidential Unit Citation, the Bronze Star, three Purple Hearts, the*

Combat Infantryman Badge, the POW Medal, and numerous other ribbons and medals. His son has written a book on his father's life, entitled Courage on Bataan and Beyond. *See his websites: www.powbook.com and www.harrisonheritage.com/adbc/ortega.htm*

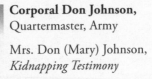

Corporal Don Johnson,
Quartermaster, Army

Mrs. Don (Mary) Johnson,
Kidnapping Testimony

Author's Note: Corporal Don Johnson, Quartermaster, served in the Army. He and his wife, Mary, lived in Germany during 1954 and 1955. Sometimes, one of the greatest fears of a military family is having a family member kidnapped. This is the story of Mary's experience; it is a dramatic account of the power of God's deliverance and protection. Mary tells in her own words the testimony of her kidnapping miracle.

After returning from a five-day Red Brangus cow sale where my husband and I also met our daughter to buy clothes for our soon-to-be-born first grandchild, I had got an early start that morning to catch up on my chores. We live twelve miles out in the country, so I was surprised to be interrupted by a young man in an old van—supposedly lost—asking for a drink of water.

The pretense was over when he pulled a gun and told me to get in the car. My surprised scream was soon stifled when he threatened my life if I did that again. I was thrown into the back of the van, where a man wearing a nylon stocking on his head put athletic tape over my mouth and my hands, and covered my head with a black windbreaker. Black shag carpet covered the sides, floor, and roof of the van. The windows were covered with black curtains.

I couldn't tell where they were taking me. I know

we crossed railroad tracks and ended up on a gravel road. I had never been so frightened in my life. All I could think about was that I was soon to be fifty—soon to be a grandmother—and I wasn't sure I would live to see either my birthday or my first grandchild.

But my greatest fear was being raped. Finally, however, I came to my senses and started claiming my spiritual covenant promise of protection. I suddenly realized that I was a child of God—fear was of the devil—and I had the protection of God on my life.

By this time we had stopped. With a wool cap pulled down over my face, I was led over a barbed-wire fence and across a pasture to an old, abandoned ranch house where I was handcuffed to the bathroom pipes.

One of my kidnappers asked, "What would be the best way to get your husband to cooperate without alerting the police?" Then I was warned that if he went to the police he would never see me again—alive! A phone call with all the usual kidnapping threats and instructions was planned, and then I was left to my dilemma.

Still quoting my promises, singing hymns of deliverance, and thanking God, I was frantically working to get the pipes loose, but they wouldn't budge. God said in Psalm 91:15: "In your day of trouble, call upon Me and I will answer." I started praying, "Lord, I am calling on You! I can't do this, but You can. Show me a way to get loose."

Then for the first time I noticed a tiny pipe coming up the back of the sink. I don't have any idea how I was able to break through, but I know it was a miracle because the FBI agent couldn't believe I was able to do what I did.

Feeling sure the kidnappers would make their call to Don and be back shortly, I was out the back door and over the fence in no time. I had no idea where I was, but I was confident God would get me where I needed to be. Twelve miles later I came to a house with every door locked except the front door. I later found out the owner never left her doors unlocked, except on this particular day. After several calls I got the sheriff on his way to pick me up, but my husband had already left for Goldthwaite, Texas, with the ransom money.

The kidnappers skipped the first meeting but called at 12:30 that night with a new appointed place to meet in Austin, Texas. Obviously, they didn't know I had escaped. This time it was the Texas Rangers who met and took the first man into custody; later, the second one was apprehended. I was called to Austin by the FBI to pick him out of a lineup. All I asked was for the men in the lineup to wear a ballcap and say, "Would you get me a glass of water?" With that, I was able to successfully pick him out of the group and my job was over.

I thank God for His covenant of protection in Psalm 91. We do not have to be afraid of the "terror of what man can do to us—it will not approach us."

Author's Note: *The man who was convicted of this crime was no amateur criminal. According to police, he'd had a habitual crime problem since his youth and had previously been convicted and imprisoned for robbery, indecency, and sexual assault. For this present offense he was sentenced to ninety-nine years in prison.*

The sheriff told Mary Johnson they had never had anyone in their local jail as malicious as this man. The

FBI was shocked that Mary was able to escape, and even more shocked that she had not been beaten, raped, or murdered. One of the FBI agents said, "We cannot believe we are sitting here today with you and you are alive and well." Obviously, very few people understand the power of this wonderful covenant.

Rick Johnson, Vietnam

In 1966 I decided to drop out of College and join the Marine Corps so I could go to Vietnam. The Marines were looking for pilots and wanted me to go to flight school, but I was determined to be an infantry grunt. To this day, I still don't know why.

I completed my training and got orders to go to Vietnam just as I had requested. Just before leaving home, my fiancé's mother, Erma Carroll, asked me to sit down so she could read something to me. She read Psalm 91 and told me how much it meant to her, and that the Lord had put it on her heart to read that Scripture to me before I left.

I was not familiar with it but I remembered where it was and read it from time to time. I grew up in a Christian home but was not familiar with standing on the Word and declaring the Word. God's faithfulness to watch over His Word and perform it (Jeremiah 1:12) even reaches beyond our ignorance, and He did just that for me.

Several months later I was able to read the daily Bible reading selection on my birthday; it was Psalm 91! God is awesome. My future mother-in-law back home also saw that Psalm 91 was printed in the daily Bible reading, along with my birthday, and knew that it was just another sign that I was being protected.

I have lots of memories of Vietnam. I had a great time serving there and believed in what we were doing, trying to help people become free. There were many times when I was aware that the Lord was preserving my life. Once another soldier standing a foot away from me was shot by a sniper; once a mortar round landed ten feet in front of me and didn't detonate; once a grenade blew up less than ten feet from where I was standing, fully erect, and I was not hit.

However, I want to share with you in a little more detail a particular experience that illustrates God's protection over me. In the spring of 1967, the lonely combat base at Khe Sanh, just south of the DMZ, was like most other places in Vietnam—unknown to the world, although not for long. We landed at the airstrip and were immediately ordered to join a number of other Marine companies strung along the narrow footpaths. Our job was to search through the rugged mountainous terrain for the North Vietnamese Army units who had been assigned to wipe Khe Sanh off the map.

Our first day out we were approaching hill 861. I was stepping over the bloated body of a three-days-dead Marine, thinking something was very wrong. Marines never leave anyone behind. For this body to be lying exposed on a lonely, recently burned and blasted hill, was more than wrong. I had never seen this before. We all knew something was up and were "beyond" fully alert.

Just then, the NVA (North Vietnamese) opened fire on us. I carried the PRC-25 radio for the Platoon leader, who was immediately in front of me. In the initial volley of fire, the Lance Corporal in front of the lieutenant was hit badly and the man behind me had his left arm shattered. The primary goal in the first shots of an ambush is to take out the radio man and the man next to him (communications and leadership). So there was no doubt in my mind about who had been in the gunner's sights when he pulled the trigger.

I rolled left and the Lieutenant rolled right as we dove for cover that simply did not exist. We had just passed the crest of a hill that had been hit with napalm, leaving less than two inches of grassy stubble. We were exposed. We both scrambled back to allow the top of the small hill to provide a semblance of cover.

The company commander wanted a report, so I passed the handset to the Lieutenant. The lead elements of our platoon were cut off from us in a deep, steep ravine, dividing the hill where the enemy was concealed in bunkers from the hill we were on. Our Staff Sergeant, who was with the other group, organized an assault and had all the men pull the pins on their grenades, ready to storm the hill in front of us. Our rocket launcher team, headed up by a Christian, was beside the Lieutenant and me, fully exposed, firing on the enemy positions.

When he ran out of rocket ammunition, the team leader yelled to the wounded Lance Corporal in front of us, who still lay fully exposed to the enemy, "I'm coming to get you!" With that, we all started firing ferociously with our rifles, to cover our buddies, and all three of our machine gunners appeared and stood fully erect, shoulder-to-shoulder, firing from the hip to cover this heroic rescue.

This is the most beautiful sight anyone could ever hope to have etched in his memory. I can still see the smoke, fire, and brass spewing from these guns as the wounded man was carried, arms and legs dangling, over the top of the hill to a waiting corpsman who would tend to his multiple wounds.

A little later, I found myself still pinned down,

talking on the radio behind a log that was about eight inches in diameter. Another buddy piled in on top of me, wanting to get into one more good fight before he left for home. I described to him what he would see when he looked up, and that the most accurate fire was from the bunker just to the right of the small, lone tree across from us. Not realizing that the gunner was still trying to take me out, since I had the radio, and that he was, at that moment, sighted in on my radio antenna that stuck up from my position, my friend raised his head to look. Three shots from the enemy's automatic weapon hit him in the forehead about an inch below the rim of his helmet and he fell lifeless onto me. He saved my life with that move. He didn't do it on purpose, but he saved my life. I was just through talking on the radio and was getting ready to do exactly what he had just done.

I looked for years on the Vietnam Memorial Wall trying to find the name of the badly wounded Lance Corporal; it didn't make sense that he lived with wounds that severe. I couldn't find it. The Corporal's name is there—I wish it wasn't. When I see his name or recite this story, it brings up powerful emotions in me even thirty-nine years later. I'm thankful that the Lord's mercy endures forever, including today. Two years ago, I was looking at a military site and found that our wounded Lance Corporal had signed the guest book. I wrote to him; it turns out that he died twice on the operating table and lost a limb, but he's alive. Praise the Lord, he made it!

I've found fifty-four men I actually served with in Vietnam. We have reorganized our Battalion Landing Team and I have the privilege of serving as the chaplain. We've found over a thousand who served in our battalion, and we get together each year. Our purpose is to reach out to our brothers and rescue them. Many are still fighting the war today, and we have often been able to touch them and help.

Psalm 91 has grown more precious every year. My wife of thirty-eight years and I have grown to love the Lord Jesus in a dimension that we didn't know existed. We have learned that the Word is a Person (Revelation 19:13; John 1:1–3), and we have fallen in love with Him more than we knew we could, and we've only just begun. I am convinced that God's Covenant Psalm 91, spoken over me, and therefore watching over me, is the only reason I am alive today.

The Lord speaks to me with His tender voice, usually when I'm quiet and not being interrupted. It's not unusual for Him to give me a reference from Psalm 91 and show me another time or another way in which He "saved and rescued me" when I wasn't even aware. It just makes me love Him more and be even more thankful.

I don't believe my life has been spared any more than any other person. Even people who will never walk across a battlefield have an enemy who is out to kill and destroy them. We all need to be rescued every day. We all have protection available every day. Glory to God in the highest. Holy, holy, holy is His name!

Author's Note: Corporal Ira "Rick" Johnson saw over two hundred combat days with 3rd Battalion, 9th Marine Regiment, 3rd Marine Division, in the Republic of Vietnam from August 1966 until September 1967. He has been awarded the Bronze Star with combat V for valor, the Purple Heart for wounds received in action, and several other medals for combat service while serving in the Marine Corps. He and his wife now live in Bradenton Florida where he serves as Property Operations Manager at Bradenton Missionary Village.

Andrew Wommack
Specialist, First Class, Vietnam

My deployment in Vietnam extended from January 1970 through the end of February 1971. I served in the 196th Infantry Brigade as an assistant to the chaplain. I was well aware of the security God had provided through His protection covenant of Psalm 91, and I knew it was just as reliable in wartime as in peace time, but I also knew it needed to be seriously appropriated by faith in this new hostile environment. I will be sharing four instances that immediately come to mind with respect to God's faithfulness to this Psalm 91 covenant of protection.

It was against regulations to leave the military base at brigade level without going in convoy with an armored personnel carrier before and behind. My captain, however, was a chaplain, and chaplains could do pretty much what they wanted to do. One day he decided to go out on the countryside and visit a Vietnamese pastor. Against regulations I got a jeep out of the motor pool and we got off the main highway and drove out of the area to find this man. Since it was against regulations it was more than a bit risky—here was an American jeep and two American soldiers out in the middle of Vietnam with no protection around.

After visiting with the pastor for about thirty minutes or so, the chaplain asked him, "Is there any Viet Cong activity around here?" The pastor assured him there was a great deal of Viet Cong activity. He had us look out the window to a long building directly across the street, which he said was a Viet Cong headquarters.

Needless to say, there were Viet Cong walking around with AK-47s—the Russian-made weapon. They were not American friendly and they were right across the street, with our jeep in plain sight. The chaplain got so scared that all he wanted was to get out of there as quickly as possible. There we were— two Americans in uniform, in an Army jeep, driving through these Vietnamese guards who had AK-47s on their shoulders. We know they saw us because, as we drove they would get out of the way of the jeep and let us pass. They didn't say a thing to us and never pointed a weapon at us as we drove right through the midst of them. There were about six of them, and they simply parted as we drove on by.

The whole thing was so incomprehensible that the chaplain and I just looked at each other, speechless. I'm not sure what happened. There is no telling what God did to enable us to get out of there alive. There is no natural explanation for those Viet Cong not to have taken us captive or killed us on the spot, except for one thing.

> He will cover you with His pinions,
> and under His wings you may seek
> refuge; His faithfulness is a shield
> and bulwark. (Psalm 91:4)

Another time I was driving from Da Nang to my headquarters some sixty miles south. It was a paved highway that went north and south through Vietnam. Sometimes people drove alone, but it was against regulations and was especially dangerous when one drove through towns, because there were people everywhere. Given this sea of people around your vehicle, you were often forced to slow down almost to a stop, and it was not uncommon for someone to wrap a cloth around a hand grenade, pull the pin and throw it into the gas tank. The gas would eat the rag away, releasing the handle and blowing up the gas tank.

I had been a little apprehensive about getting through so my faith was just a little shaky. I specifically remember going across a huge bridge just outside the town, because I was praying and singing praises to God for His divine protection in getting me through. I also remember hearing a lot of gunfire, but I didn't think much about it because gunfire was quite common— just something you learned to live with.

But then, as I continued south on Highway 1, in less than ten minutes after crossing the bridge I saw a convoy and another chaplain's assistant who was a friend of mine going north. I waved at him and went on. Later I met this same guy in Da Nang, who said, "How did you get across the bridge right outside that town?"

"I just drove across it. Why?" Then he told me that by the time they got to the bridge, less than ten minutes after I had crossed it, the convoy was stopped because of all the Vietnamese and American bodies they had piled up that had been killed. It turned out the Viet Cong had been on one side of the bridge, the Americans on the other side, and while I was just singing and worshiping the Lord I had driven across right through the middle of the firefight. I was totally unaware I was driving through a huge gun battle, and I never got touched.

A thousand may fall at your side
and ten thousand at your right
hand, but it shall not approach you.
(Psalm 91:7)

I experienced another supernatural protection
when I was with more than a hundred other men on
a landing zone located about forty-five miles from the
nearest U.S. emplacement. I was asleep one night while
some of our guys were practice-firing from a U.S. Huey
helicopter. They had asked for grid coordinates but had
gotten the wrong grid cord, so this Huey Cobra began
firing on our hill. They fired a 50-caliber machine gun
at our bunker, made of two layers of 4x12s on top
and two layers of sand bags—and those rounds went
through our bunker right beside my bed.

I narrowly escaped being killed by friendly fire
that night, yet when I woke up the next morning
I didn't know anything had happened. When we
looked, however, we could see where the bullets had
come through. Several people on our hill were killed
from that accident, and the bullets came within a few
feet of me, but none of them touched me.

I will not be afraid of the arrows
[bullets]…they will not come near
me. (Psalm 91:5–7)

Another time, when I pulled bunker duty on
LZ west, there was a bunker out on a finger of that
441-meter hill. The hill was so steep that it was almost
impregnable, except for only one way up. That was
where this bunker was located, blocking the route
from the bottom. It was sort of an outpost, and I

was out there with three other guys, pulling bunker guard.

I pulled the first guard duty, and there was another guy who sat up on top with me. He was a Puerto Rican who had been drafted and didn't speak any English. I tried talking to him and all he would say was, "Forty days."

"Have you been in the country forty days?" I asked, and he said it again: "Forty days." I couldn't talk to him so I pulled my four-hour bunker guard and then I lay on top of the bunker and went to sleep. We were supposed to stay there until six, but when I woke up about three or four in the morning everyone was gone. I didn't know what had happened, so I finished up the bunker guard until six o'clock and then headed up the hill.

At that point the chaplain met me and asked if I was all right. "What are you talking about?" I said.

It turned out that, while I was sleeping right beside this Puerto Rican, he had gone crazy and shot off every M-16 round he had—hundreds of them. He threw more than a hundred hand grenades. He shot a hundred or so M-69 grenade launchers, and he fired off four or five claymore mines. This guy was literally crazy, and the other guys who were pulling bunker guard with us got scared and ran up the hill, while he was still shooting and throwing hand grenades.

They were ready to blow him away because they didn't know what on earth he was doing, and they knew he had a tremendous amount of ammunition. But they also knew I was still down there so they couldn't do anything. The uncanny part is that I slept through the whole thing—obviously, God protected me through the whole ordeal.

For He will give His angels charge
concerning you, to guard you in all
your ways. (Psalm 91:11)

Probably the one incident that made the greatest impact on me, twenty years after the fact, was the time when the chaplain and I went out to an LZ right on the Laotian border. It was a temporary fire support base with probably no more than fifty people on this little hill, and they had put some mortars and some artillery there to support the troops that were down in the valley, fighting. During a service the chaplain held, dozens of mortar rounds began to hit directly within the perimeters of this very small building we were in.

In fact, we took a number of direct mortar hits because the hill was being assaulted. I had my M-16 out. I didn't use it, but we were so close that I could actually see the fire from the muzzles of the Vietnamese weapons. Because the chaplain wasn't expendable they sent a chopper. They wanted to get him out of there and I was told to go with him.

Within an hour of the time we left, that whole place was overrun. I honestly didn't think much about it at the time because it was just another day in Vietnam, but several years later something happened to let me know how supernaturally God had intervened. I was in Chicago and a man gave me a book in which he and eleven other people had described their Vietnam experiences. His testimony was really powerful, so I started reading the others and discovered three of them were there at the same time I was.

Two of them were from my division, and one of them told about a battle fought on a fire support base right on the Laotian border. He was one of the very few people who lived through this particular ordeal. I realized he had to have been talking about the exact same battle where I was.

The thing that affected me so much was that he wrote it from an unbeliever's perspective. At the time he wrote it he wasn't born again, and he described the terror that engulfed him. When I was there I loved God with all of my heart so I was fine if the Lord was ready to take me home—not because I was discouraged with the war, but because I was so in love with the Lord I was ready to meet Him at any time.

Therefore, when we were in that situation and it looked as though we were going to be overrun, instead of fear I was feeling the peace of God and excitement that "today could be the day I am going to see my Lord."

As it turned out, before it was over the hill was overrun and practically every person there was killed. I remember watching the fire coming from their weapons and feeling nothing at the time except a love for those poor, lost souls who were headed for hell. It was like I had a bubble around me, and I never experienced fear because my heart was so filled with peace.

But twenty years after the war, as I read that testimony of what I believe to be the same battle I was involved in, I had a flashback and I saw through the eyes of an unbeliever what it was like to go through that conflict without being in relationship with God. So twenty years after being out of Vietnam, I had panic and terror hit me so hard it took me months to deal with it and get over the fear. God opened a curtain and let me see how it would have been had I not known Him intimately. I thank God for His shield that protects us mentally and emotionally, as well as physically.

> He who dwells in the shelter of the Most High will abide under the shadow of the Almighty. (Psalm 91:1)

> Because he [Andrew] has loved Me, therefore I will deliver him; I will set him securely on high, because he has known My name. (Psalm 91:14)

After that experience I realized what an advantage I had while I was in Vietnam. I was truly seated together with Him, watching the war from a much higher perspective—in His shelter where there is no fear. I thank God that I knew Him. I shudder to think what it must have been like for those who were fighting with me who didn't know God in an intimate way.

> Truly He has never left me, nor forsaken me. (Hebrews 13:5)

Author's Note: For more than three decades, Andrew Wommack has traveled America and the rest of the world, teaching the truth of the Gospel. For more information, Andrew Wommack's ministry can be contacted at 719-635-1111, or at www.awmi.net.

James Crow, DDS
Captain, U.S. Air Force

Julie's miracle, as told by her father

Author's note: *Dr. James Crow was on inactive status as a first lieutenant for four years while he was in dental school, and went on active duty the summer of 1971 after graduation. He was active as a captain in the USAF near Lubbuck, Texas, at Reese Air Force training base in the medical unit for two years. He received an honorable discharge in the summer of 1973. This is the story of his daughter.*

Julie's ordeal began in May 1983 while she attended a friend's birthday party in the country. Julie had ridden horses with her grandfather for nearly nine of her ten years, so when they asked who wanted to ride she jumped at the chance. But a ten-year-old riding bareback on a grown horse has very little to hold onto—so when the horse began to run she slipped under its belly. Between the rocks and the hooves she received a very serious head injury.

When we arrived at the hospital a physician friend tried to be a buffer for us before we saw our daughter. He warned us that she was in very serious condition and that the hospital was already making arrangements to have her transported to the nearest large city for treatment. Even with his attempt to prepare us we were still not anywhere close to being ready for what we saw. The right side of her head was swollen literally to the size of a volleyball, both eyes were swollen shut, and her hair and face were drenched in blood. There was no way we could have recognized her.

I need, at this point, to interject some crucial information. Through the teachings of Kenneth Copeland of Copeland Ministries in Fort Worth, I had started doing a great deal of study on healing and faith. Jesus and I had spent a lot of time alone together, during which I received the baptism of the Holy Spirit, and the Lord became very personal to me. And our church was strong on believing that Jesus is still the "Healer."

I can truly say that from the instant I first saw Julie's condition, I called on Jesus and totally expected that His healing power and His promises in Psalm 91 would bring her through. I'm glad I didn't have to analyze the situation, but we all knew it was so bad that we had to have a miracle. Even before the ambulance reached the hospital, there was a growing network of believers who were interceding.

In addition to the driver, there were two paramedics in the back of the ambulance with Julie and one in the front between the driver and me. I prayed all the way—just in a whisper—almost oblivious to the others in the cab. I remember thanking Jesus for her healing and telling Satan that he couldn't have Julie—that she was a child of God and had been dedicated to the Lord from birth. For the entire eighty-five miles I never stopped claiming her healing. I didn't get loud—I knew I was being heard in both realms of the spirit.

Then, somewhere just this side of Abilene, the paramedics slid the panel open between the back and the cab area and said something to the driver. We had been going fairly fast all the way, but at this point the driver put on his siren and sped the rest of the way to the hospital. I found out later that Julie had lost all vital signs and could not be revived. I'm not sure how long she had no vital signs, but it was more than minutes. I learned that life came back into her body about the time we came to the edge of town.

While all this was happening, my brother-in-law, who was an elder in our church, was about forty-five minutes behind us in his car. On the way he felt that God told him that Julie had died, and God asked him if he would be willing to lie across her body like the prophet Elisha had done with the little boy in 2 Kings 4:34 to bring him back to life. Realizing this meant he would most likely have to push his way past the doctors and nurses and look very foolish, he said that he wrestled within himself for several minutes before knowing without a doubt that he was willing to do it. The moment the commitment was made, he felt God told him Julie would be all right.

We later backtracked to the place where he was en route during this confrontation with God. According to our calculations, the ambulance would have been coming into the city limits just about the time God told him that Julie would be all right. That was when her vital signs returned.

Upon our arrival Julie was immediately taken in for a CAT scan. When the doctor got the results he realized that her skull had been cracked like an egg, with so many complications that he gave us no hope whatsoever. Someone asked him if there would be brain damage.

"Parents always want to ask about brain damage. Your concern needs to be whether she will live through the night, but if she does live, yes, there will be extensive brain damage."

I was not arrogant, but I denied each negative statement from anyone who was not standing in faith with us. The doctor was obviously perturbed, but I'm sure he just thought we were in denial. He just didn't realize where our denial was coming from. To the doctor's total surprise, Julie did live through the night. We kept healing Scriptures on her pillow at all times and held her and spoke love to her continuously. My wife had the astronomical job of cleaning the dried blood from her hair and untangling it—speaking healing and quoting Psalm 91 over her the whole time.

We were told that we were in for a long stay, but my frustration was that Julie wasn't climbing out of the bed the next day, ready to go home. God must have given me a gift of faith because I was ready for a Lazarus healing. We began to notice that, miraculously, nearly every timetable we were given was accomplished seven times faster. At first we thought it was a neat coincidence, until it continued way beyond any possibility of chance.

During the hospital stay of only nine days, we saw our miracle unfold. Julie's physical damage continued to heal at a supernatural rate. The swelling went down, her color returned to normal, and her mental activity went from bizarre to normal. Every day was a miracle. There were other patients in the hospital with head injuries, seemingly not nearly as serious as Julie's, who had been there six months and more. Many of them were just learning how to walk and talk again.

During the next few days we saw Julie protected by Jesus while He was accomplishing her healing. It was as if her body was left on the hospital bed to go through the healing while Julie herself—her soul, maybe; her spirit for sure—seemed to retreat inside to be cuddled by Jesus until the healing process was complete. For the first several days after the accident we could not recognize anything about her that reminded us of our Julie. Then a little at a time we saw her return until she was totally back to normal. We could almost see the healing taking place before our very eyes. The nurses were amazed. They all called her their "miracle girl."

Even our hardcore neurosurgeon—without giving credit to God—said that her recovery couldn't be explained. He saw us praying and standing and believing day after day, and because of the results unfolding before his very eyes he could not very easily have gone home and called us a bunch of kooks.

On the night of the accident we had been told that, in addition to the brain damage, there would be considerable loss of hearing since the mastoid bone had been part of the skull fracture. They were also quite sure that the optic nerve had been damaged, which we were told would cause either total—or at least partial—loss of eyesight. When Julie was dismissed only nine days after entering the hospital, the only outward sign of the accident was that her right eye was still a little bloodshot.

She went home with no brain damage and no loss of eyesight (20/20 vision). On the day of her release, however, the attending physician—even after watching her miraculous recovery—still insisted, "*There will be a hearing loss,*" and he instructed us to take her to the audiologist in July. We did that, only to be told that she had perfect hearing. We thank Jesus for what He did on the cross for each one of us, and for His wonderful promises in Psalm 91.

Author's Note: *Julie and her husband, Rocky, live in San Antonio, Texas, where Julie works as a dental hygienist.*

Rene Hood of Bangs, Texas
Specialist, Fourth Class, U.S. Army

Author's note: Rene Hood joined the army after graduating from H. D. Woodson High School in Washington DC at the age of sixteen. While at military school at Fort Harrison, for training in finances and accounting, she played on the girl's basketball team, where she became the VIP and led her team to the championship. That earned her honors in the military newspaper. She served in the U.S. Army for two years, from 1976 to 1978—part of which was spent in Europe. She attained the ranking of Specialist Fourth Class and was honorably discharged.

My testimony begins in July 1998. At this point in my life I had eaten almost nothing for approximately two months, yet I continued to gain weight. I could not go outside in the direct sunlight for any length of time without my face becoming irritated so badly that, if you placed your hand on my face, the print of your hand would remain there. I had also begun to develop black spots on my face, arms and legs. Later a red rash appeared on my face and throughout my body. Bruises would appear without my falling or having been hit.

During the month of July, my energy level was so low it was a challenge to just clean the bathtub after bathing. My body became racked with pain, even when I tried performing a task as simple as brushing my teeth. One particular night is still fresh in my memory. For the previous week or so, I had been choking when I'd lie down at night. This night was the same, but when I got up that morning I made the shocking discovery that I couldn't perform normal bodily functions. Knowing something had to be done quickly, I made an immediate appointment with my regular doctor, who examined me and then referred me to Scott and White Hospital, to see Dr. Nichols, a nephrologist. The night prior to my seeing Dr. Nichols, my body aches had reached a new level. I had a fever of 103 degrees or more. I felt like my brain was frying. I would lie on my bathroom floor, in misery. My brown body transformed before my eyes into a gray color, covered with perspiration and rolled up in a fetal position.

I told the Lord it would be so easy to give up the ghost and just go home to be with Him, but I also said, "Lord, I know You are not finished with me. Lord, I hurt so badly and yet I know there are people out there You have called me to touch. My kids need me! I know I am walking in the valley of the shadow of death, but I will fear no evil. You promised me, Lord, in Psalm 91 that only with my eyes would I see the reward of the wicked—that a thousand would fall at my side and ten thousand at my right hand, but it would not come nigh me."

At that point my eighteen-year-old daughter took me to Temple hospital. I was so weak I could barely walk. After a twenty-five-minute examination, the nephrologist, with no bedside manner and no sense of caring, said, "You are in the last stages of lupus and going to die. I give you three months and you will just go 'poop.'"

I was very angry that he would speak such words to me in the presence of my daughter, without any sensitivity. Then he said, "It will not be easy because you will be in a lot of pain, but [as he pointed to my daughter] she's big enough—she can take care of herself."

Then he walked out the door, at which point I looked at my daughter and assured her that "Mom is not going anywhere!"

I was hospitalized, running a high fever, and unable to eat. I would have involuntary shakes I couldn't control, and my right lung had collapsed because of the massive amounts of protein my kidneys were now throwing into my system. I looked like a seven-months-pregnant woman. My kidneys were shutting down, my aching joints were swollen, and the doctors had found a mass on my liver.

After twelve days, during which they made one mistake after another and caused me more suffering without my getting any better, I asked my daughter to help me dress and take me back home to Bangs, Texas, because God was going to give me a miracle.

I am a living testimony of God's faithfulness to His promises. I went to my parents' house where I would sit up and walk as well as I could, reminding God of what He had promised "You will not be afraid of the deadly pestilence. It will not approach you."

My local doctor would call and remind me that those specialists said I was dying and I needed to be in a hospital. I wouldn't! I couldn't! I knew "Greater is He that is in me than he that is in the world." I had a supernatural peace that I was well and the healing would manifest itself soon—so I kept pressing.

Since I would not go back to the hospital, and my

condition (based on what could be seen) was no better, my doctor encouraged me to go to a nephrologist in Abilene, Texas. I finally agreed but refused the medicine because of the side effects. Not one doctor gave me one ounce of hope, but I was determined to receive the healing Christ had provided.

Then the miracle very slowly began to manifest. During the next few months I gradually started feeling better, and my strength started returning—slowly but surely. Finally after seeing the Abilene doctor for two months and once again being put through a battery of tests, he said, "I'm looking at your paperwork and I'm looking at you. If you had let us do what we wanted to do—and you wouldn't—we doctors would be patting ourselves on the back, saying we had gotten you in remission. All I can say is—whatever you have been doing, just keep doing it." Then he told me I was a miracle.

My doctor had a liver specialist meet me at the Brownwood hospital, and after a CAT scan and two sonograms, he could not find any mass in my liver. I was then sent to a blood specialist, and after reading the reports he repeated twice that I was "a wonder." I have seen many Christmases since being told I would not even live to see the one at the end of 1998.

My prison ministry didn't suffer and souls continue to be saved, delivered, and set free because I abided in God's Word and trusted Him to be faithful. I expect to have a book out soon, called *Being Found in His Word*. We all need to be in His Word, refusing no matter what to be driven from His promises.

I know this battle and subsequent victory give honor to a faithful, loving, and caring God who desires to be embraced by each one of us.

CH (LTC) James H. Finn
Connecticut Army National Guard

After the 1st Cavalry Division deployed to Saudi Arabia for Operation Desert Shield, the 544th Maintenance Battalion was redesignated the 544th Corps Support Battalion, leaving Fort Hood on October 31, 1990. During the lockdown in the 13th COSCOM Gymnasium, "Spiritual MREs" were handed to each soldier boarding the buses headed for the airfield. Small Bibles, Jewish Scriptures, and Korans filled the packets for the soldiers of various faiths along with other corresponding literature. The one item all the packets had in common was Psalm 91 cards.

Just before the headquarters' company left, the Battalion Commander, LTC Richard Hall, asked me to pray. All I remember of the prayer are the major parts of Psalm 91, which I offered to the Lord for protection over all the soldiers. I then closed with, "I claim Psalm 91, and Lord, please bring all our soldiers back safely to the United States."

After arriving in Saudi Arabia, the 544th was assigned various companies and swelled to 1,500 personnel. We moved out into the desert where a revival broke out, and various soldiers in each of our companies volunteered as Religious Operations Coordinators (ROC). The Battalion was divided into two missions for fuel and for ammunition: Task Force Cofer and Task Force Hart. During convoy training operations, some personnel throughout the Battalion were claiming Psalm 91, while some personnel I counseled claimed the two missions would end in disaster. The accusation was that dozens would die when the 1st Cavalry began combat operations, leaving the task forces abandoned in Iraq with no escort.

One dusty night we held a worship service in our Quartermaster Company from San Antonio, simultaneous with the convoy training. We prayed, as we did at every Battalion service, for continued safety, wisdom, and God's protection. At the end of the service, one of the truck drivers came limping into the mess hall chapel and said, "God was with me tonight. Ouch!! I'm bruised up, but I still got my legs." He explained that in the dusty dark the truck in front of him got stuck in the sand, so he stopped. He set his brake and got out to see what he could do for the driver in front, not realizing that the truck behind had not seen his brake lights and was still moving.

The trucks had been making a tight right turn around a hill, so to get to the one that was stuck he had to walk in front of his own vehicle just as the third truck rear-ended his. The bumper knocked him down and the 915 rolled over both his legs. But instead of having them crushed he was pushed down through the desert crust and stuck, so that he couldn't move. The driver got out and found him buried up to his waist. The convoy backed up the trucks and dug him out. On any other road surface he would have been a double amputee.

A few days later the ground war, Operation Desert Storm, was launched. Two convoys full of fuel and ammunition chased the 1st Cavalry Division across the desert. By midday the sun was at its highest and they were nearing their first site to set up the transfer points. Suddenly, a white pickup truck rose over a large dune near the fuel convoy. When the truck stopped only a couple hundred yards from the tankers, a man with an RPG (Rocket Propelled Grenade) came up over the cab, fired and pounded the truck to get moving. As the RPG sizzled toward the convoy, dozens of soldiers stopped, then dove out of their trucks and opened fire on the pickup. The RPG slammed full speed into the side of a five-thousand-gallon tank truck with a loud "bonk," then flew off and landed in the sand, leaving a dent the size and depth of a Kevlar helmet. Everyone was amazed that nothing had exploded, and one brave soldier went to look at the RPG. The report later stated that the arming pin had not been pulled. Praise God for His protecting power.

After the four-day ground war ended, with numerous "close calls," the 544th CSB regrouped with no fatalities and only one Purple Heart. Apparently one of our personnel was assisting with a supply route recon (we thought he was souvenir hunting) and drove a Hummer too close to a magnetic mine buried in the wall of a twenty-foot sand berm. The mine exploded causing two flat tires, destroying the front and rear right fenders, but leaving no fatalities. Shrapnel struck the right calves of both right-side passengers, but no one else was injured other than the ringing in their ears. My opinion was that protecting angels were next to the vehicle and the shrapnel had gone through their legs. I believe God has a sense of humor even in the midst of combat chaos.

After returning to the states and preparing for redeployment, we did have one death in our battalion. He was a cargo escort who accompanied our vehicles on the ship back to the States. He disappeared after the ship docked in the port of Houston. A thorough search was conducted, of the port and the ship, but he was nowhere to be found. Three days after the ship unloaded and left port, his body came floating to the surface. The Lord has not told me the "why" of his death, and foul play was not ruled out. However, the Lord had honored our prayer and brought every soldier safely back to the United States.

Captain Thomas H. Bond, Jr.
U.S. Navy

During the summer of 2004, my family was transferred from a sea duty assignment in Florida to shore duty in Washington DC. Let me share with you the process of how God provided a home for us here in the DC area.

Several months before we moved from Florida we started house hunting in the DC area. We did not want to buy a house or pay the exorbitant rent for a house that would permit a seven-children, home schooling family to have a bit of elbow room.

I made inquiries by phone and almost made a trip up to scope out the prospects before I left for a two-month underway period in the eastern Atlantic in June and July. No joy. No military quarters were available that would meet our needs. The rental market had very expensive offerings which were long commuting distances away from my place of work. Against this I knew that, when I returned home in late July, we would have a short time to pack up and move north before my war college class started in the second week of August. There would be no time to find a place to live before we arrived.

During the previous year, Lorraine and I read the book *Those Who Trust in the Lord Shall Not Be Disappointed,* by Peggy Joyce Ruth. Primarily, it was about how the Lord is faithful to His Word, and it related testimony after testimony telling how she and her family took the Lord seriously about His ability to meet their needs in specific ways. In particular, they were not disappointed in His miraculous provision of a home in a unique way. The book was a catalyst for our faith.

In May, Lorraine and I decided to trust the Lord to provide us a place to live in the Washington DC area. We got the whole family around the kitchen table and set up the whiteboard to capture ideas. I asked each person in the family to list our needs and desires for a home in our next duty station. We also listed ministry areas in which we have been led to serve as a family and to which our home situation would serve us in complementary fashion.

In total we listed over thirty desires and needs for our home, most of which were desires. From the list I wrote up a document that specifically covenanted with the Lord about our move to Washington DC, detailing how our family would be used of the Lord in His purposes.

A key promise we trusted in came from Psalm 37:5, "Commit your way to the Lord, trust also in Him, and He will do it." We prayed frequently as a family, lifting this compact up to the Lord, reminding Him that we trusted Him to meet our needs and thanking Him for what He would do.

We packed up and drove from Florida at the end of July, without any worldly reason to hope we would find the house we needed. We arrived at the Anacostia Navy housing office in Washington DC on August 2 and were told what we had heard before. They had no available large quarters for us, so they asked if we would like to see the rental market listing. In response I asked if there might be something unusual available—could they think "out-of-the-box" about other options? Perhaps something on a military base, farther out from Washington DC.

The lady called several different distant bases with no success. Then she called the Navy base at Indian Head in Maryland, about forty-five minutes south of downtown Washington. Her eyes brightened as she spoke on the phone. Sure enough, they had a big house that was available now—it was an old house and had eight bedrooms. I was excited that this might be our provision from the Lord.

We drove immediately to Indian Head to investigate. As we drove up to the house, we noticed instantly that one of our desires had been met. It had a wraparound front porch! We also noted that another desire, almost too embarrassing to ask for, was also granted: the house had a beautiful, panoramic view of the Potomac River!

The next fifteen minutes revealed the Lord had provided every single one of the more than thirty specific requests we had laid before Him. With tears, we stopped and worshiped and thanked the Lord for His goodness to us. The cheery house we now live in is more than a hundred years old and has all the room we need. Lorraine is pleased to be able to fully unpack all our belongings for the first time in almost four years. As a bonus, it is even on a golf course with an adjacent tennis court.

Is anything too difficult for God?

Jeff and Melissa Phillips
By Crystal Phillips

Author's Note: *Every mom dreads that phone call or that letter, with news that will devastate the rest of her life. A verse every parent needs to memorize is Psalm 112:7—"I will not fear evil tidings, for my heart is steadfast, trusting in Your Word." Many times, as I head toward a ringing phone in the dead of the night, I am quoting this verse before I pick up the receiver.*

Most of us are not sure how we will react to an evil report, but I have found that faith grounded in the Word of God never fails. On January 17, 2003, I stood at San Diego Harbor watching my son, Jeff, a corporal in the U.S. Marine Corps, board the USS *Bonhomme Richard*, one of the seven warships heading for Iraq. My daughter-in-law and I were among thousands of family members treading water in a sea of emotions as we said good-bye to our loved ones. As we stood in the shadows of those gigantic ships, the feelings were ominous and foreboding.

Being told that my son could not take personal belongings on this trip, including his Bible, concerned me. I believe the Word of God is the only thing you should never leave at home. I felt somewhat consoled by the fact that Jeff had a good foundation in the Word, and I was sure that the Holy Spirit would bring Scriptures to his mind in times of need. Still, I felt that I had to "stock his arsenal" by giving him something that he could get his hands on fast. I had a book of *God's Promises* in my suitcase and the night before he shipped out I went through it and underlined specific

211

verses, but that didn't seem to be quite enough. Knowing Psalm 91, and declaring those promises over my children for years, inspired me to write out the verses inside the front cover (inserting Jeff's name throughout). I then slipped the book inside his sea bag.

Days turned to weeks before we received mail from our son. His letters spoke of gratitude for the book, tremendous faith, and encouragement for us to stay strong, followed by comments about the peace and assurance he was receiving from the Word.

About a week before President Bush declared war and we were all awakened to "Shock and Awe," a local reporter asked if he could interview me. He was writing a story to be featured in the local newspaper, covering the thoughts and feelings of families with loved ones going to war. I spoke repeatedly of my faith in God and His promises of protection. Soon after war was declared, national television brought some of the horror into our living rooms and we, along with most of the world, watched and waited. Soon afterward, the reporter called and asked me if I still felt strong in my faith after hearing that there had been American casualties. I told him "Yes!" and mentioned Psalm 91. He asked me what it was about those particular verses that gave me faith. I proceeded to read him the entire psalm.

Seven days following the declaration of war, my husband and I received a large brown envelope in the mail from the state senator's office. The address on the envelope was handwritten. Inside was a letter signed and stamped with the senator's official seal. It was a letter bearing an evil report, offering condolences for the loss of our son.

Scanning over the first few lines brought me to a *crisis of belief.* Knowing that I am not a particularly strong person in my own strength, I look back now and am quite amazed at the way I responded. Without God and the assurance of His promises, I know that I would have crumbled. But my first response was, "This is a mistake and *I will not believe this evil report!"*

At first I thought that I would ignore it and throw the letter away. Then I realized that I had to continue to declare God's promises that are written in Psalm 91. The Word of God tells us in 2 Corinthians 10:5 that the battle is in our thought life. I became more adamant about declaring God's Word and I refused to fall for the enemy's trap.

Then I thought, *I have to call the senator's office to let them know about this mistake, so other errors like this will be avoided.* Making that call led to a long wait for a response, but I refused to spread the evil report. My daughter-in-law called, but I didn't tell her. I didn't even call my husband. For approximately two hours I paced my house, vocally fighting a spiritual battle by loudly declaring the promises of God's Word. Some may disagree, not seeing the urgency of such action, but I knew that I had to line up my thoughts, my confessions, and my agreement with God's Word. I knew that my son's life was on the line! The devil had devised a plan to take my son's life, and I had no choice but to stand in the gap. I could not agree with the "evil report." The letter was a tool to cause me to give up my confession of faith so the enemy could gain the access that he desired.

The blood of Jesus and the miraculous power and protection of God that is unlimited by time or distance are what placed my son under the shadow of His almighty wings. I would not give the enemy entry! Doubters might ask if I believe that the outcome could have been different! My answer to that is another definite *"Yes!"* My son was in and out of foxholes, while dodging rounds of fire that were falling inches from his feet. Had I placed my agreement with the enemy and lost my will to trust, pray, declare, and believe God, my son might not be here today.

Finally the phone rang with a profuse apology, and confirmation that the letter had been sent by mistake. At that point I called and shared the experience with my husband, assuring him that all was well. Still, several months passed before we heard the voice of our son.

I could never adequately describe how wonderful it was on that Thursday in June, around 2 A.M., when we heard Jeff say, "What's up? I'm in Germany waiting to fly to California. Can you book me a flight to Dallas on Friday night, and will you pick me up?"

That weekend I told my two sons and their wives about the letter and brought it out for them to see. Each of them felt a sense of trauma after reading it. My two daughters-in-law and my older son, David, all said they didn't think they would have been able to handle hearing about the letter before Jeff's return.

Each member of our family knows that without God's miraculous intervention the enemy would have won. We all experienced a renewed growth in faith and trust in the promises and protection of God's Word and will always proclaim the truth and faithful delivery of Psalm 91.

Author's Note: *Crystal Phillips has a master's degree in clinical Christian counseling. She is ordained in the ministry of counseling and is a licensed pastoral counselor with the National Christian Counselor Association, as well as a licensed chemical dependency counselor in the state of Texas.*

To
Mr. + Mrs. David Phillips
Jenkins Springs Road
Brownwood, TX
76801

SENATOR TROY FRASER
P.O. Box 12068
Austin, Texas 78711

The Senate of The State of Texas

TROY FRASER

March 24, 2003

Mr. and Mrs. David Phillips
Jenkins Springs Road
Brownwood, Texas 76801

Dear Mr. and Mrs. Phillips:

Recently, I learned that you lost your son Jay while serving on the field of battle with the United States Marine Corps.

I cannot imagine the depth of your grief, and can only offer humble consolation from a grateful nation and state. I am convinced, however, that without the loyalty and bravery of your son, we would not long preserve the precious privilege of freedom.

I pray that our Heavenly Father will bring comfort and strength to your family, and that through His leadership, we will find an expedient end to this costly conflict.

Thank you for raising a young man that loved his country.

Yours, very sincerely and respectfully,

Troy Fraser
State Senator

P.O. Box 12068 • Austin, Texas 78711 • (512) 463-0124 • Dial 711 For Relay Calls

Jacob Weise
Corporal / USMC
2nd Battalion, 1st Marines

When asked to write my testimony, I wasn't sure just what to say and how much to include. For those who have already experienced the conditions brought on by combat and the imminent danger of doing our jobs in the turmoil in Iraq, you know firsthand how difficult it can be to talk about, much less to listen to someone else tell you how it is, how they "think" it is, or what they think you should be doing there.

All of that has made writing this somewhat of a struggle. Once you step away from the situation and are back on American soil, all the newly appreciated little things in life make it seem very surreal, and our first instinct is to place it all into the backs of our minds and move on with life, feeling like we have done our part and it's time to move on. I don't want to rattle on and on about all the close calls, the firefights, or the daily events that we all experienced there. Instead, I could sum up what brought me through two deployments in Iraq in one sentence. It was standing on the promises of God's Word for protection, and the prayers that were prayed over me by myself, my family, and my friends.

Just to give you a quick overview, I am an infantry machine gunner and a corporal in Golf Company, 2nd Battalion, 1st Marines. My first deployment was with the 15th MEU aboard the USS Tarawa (LHA-1) on January 6, 2003. We inserted into Iraq the first day of the war, supporting the British Royal Marines in assaulting and securing Um Quasar, the Al Faw Peninsula, and Al Basrah. Upon being detached from the British, we assaulted and secured the city of An Nasiriyah in a night operation, driving into the heart of the city along with other Marine and Army units. We remained there, patrolling and clearing the city of weapons and Anti-Coalition Forces, until we were relieved by an army unit. At that point we returned to the ship.

Our second deployment began on February 28, 2004, and involved seven months of operations in and around the city of Al Fallujah. Needless to say, this one was night-and-day different from the first operations of the war in 2003. Fallujah, unlike An Nasiriyah, was considered entirely hostile, and since we were considered to be in the restoration and rebuilding phases of operations in Iraq, the changing daily rules of engagement, the brutal, adaptive, and unpredictable enemy, and the extremely untrustworthy, unreliable Iraqi forces made Fallujah a frustrating and dangerous place to try to "win hearts and minds."

During this time, however, I always felt protected. With the exception of times we were sustaining heavy concentrations of enemy fire, I was almost always at peace in my mind, knowing that the Lord was watching over me. This was largely because before I left for boot camp, I had been taught and had taken hold of one thing—the Ninety-first Psalm and the power and promises contained in its verses that protect us from every form of evil that the enemy tries to bring against us.

When I was a college student and in the delayed-entry program, waiting to go to boot camp, I began attending a college Bible study at the home of Angelia and David Schum, at the Howard Payne University campus in Brownwood, Texas. One Tuesday night Peggy Joyce came and spoke to us, giving us one of the most thorough and complete breakdowns of Scripture I had ever heard. I normally don't retain all that much out of a message or a sermon, but her breakdown of the Ninety-first Psalm—and how to apply it to our lives—burned itself into my soul. I really had never realized just how much power the words of that psalm held. I remembered it and have since applied it to my life. My family has also locked onto the power that it holds, and I believe with all my heart that standing on that word brought me through my deployments without a scratch, either physically *or* spiritually.

I don't want to get into too many specific events because they are countless, but God's hand was constantly evident on my life, thanks to diligent prayer. His covering was miraculous, and I believe the prayers prayed over me not only protected me but also protected the Marines around me, as well. June 24, 2004, stands as a testimony to that.

My company held what we called the cloverleaf on the eastern edge of Fallujah, from June to September of 2004. This is a major highway intersection that links Ramadi, Fallujah, and Baghdad. From the first of June until the morning of the 24th, things were quiet in the city. We had one platoon there at all times, and the platoons rotated out at random times each night. The morning of the 24th started with a small concentration of small arms, mortar, and RPG fire on our positions, which were still not built or reinforced all that well, other than dirt berms and sandbags. I was at the firm base with two squads from 3rd platoon in high-back Hummers, staged to go south of the city to do humanitarian ops in the villages down along the Euphrates River and the canal.

We could hear the fighting from the Forward Operating Base (FOB), and when word came we immediately launched to go reinforce the platoon that was there in the fight. When we arrived at the cloverleaf, we had already taken one casualty, and the fire had intensified to an insane level. The buildings on the northern and western sides gave the insurgents perfect cover to lay intense, concentrated small arms and RPG fire on our positions within 250 to 500 meters. Their mortar tubes were scattered behind and within the natural cover the buildings provided, and their spotters had elevated positions from which to observe us. Initially we were not in a good spot, with limited cover and, for a couple of hours, limited fire support until we were able to get Combined Anti-Armor Team (CAAT) teams with heavy machine guns and TOWs, tanks, and air support in the form of Cobra helicopter gunships, AC-130 Spectra gunships, and F-18s.

Even as our fire support began to come on scene, the insurgents didn't let up. The Cobras were the first to arrive and hadn't been there long before one of them was shot down by what we think was a Stinger missile. I had never been under that intense a barrage of fire before. I can't really describe how I felt right then. I just remember praying the whole time I was out there. Without stopping, I was praying in the Spirit and praying the Ninety-first Psalm over us. As the tanks and eventually the AC-130s and F-18s began to level the buildings, dangerously close to our forward fighting holes, the insurgent barrage began to let up and finally lulled after an approximate six- to seven-hour exchange of fire.

At that point we had taken seven casualties, five from our company and two from the supporting units that responded. Even the circumstances of those Marines' wounds were miraculous in nature, and we didn't have a single KIA. Sniper fire had resulted in two of our Marines, including our company commander, being shot in the head. In both cases, however, the bullets had not penetrated the bone. They left only a nasty gash where the bullet traveled along the skull. Another Marine was hit in the right knee. The bullet went right under the kneecap and between the bones, leaving a clean penetration that has not impaired his full recovery. Yes, they were wounded, but I consider it miraculous compared to what the wounds could have been under the circumstances. They could just as easily have been killed or left without the use of limbs.

Over the next week, almost daily we exchanged fire with insurgents. It was intense as before and resulted in several more casualties that were again miraculous in nature, meaning that the Marines survived and recovered fully. One more Marine took an identical sniper shot to the head and it did not enter his skull. Another Marine was hit in the armpit with a .50-caliber slug from a passing Army convoy that had blown through the wall next to him. It punctured his lung and lodged in his sternum, but as with the others, he is on the road to a full recovery.

You can't call surviving a hit with a .50 cal, and recovering fully, anything *but* miraculous. The most important part of all is the fact that during all of that, as I prayed in the Spirit and rolled through the Ninety-first Psalm in my head, I never felt like anything ever came remotely close to me. In April, I had a mortar round hit so close that it killed the Marine in front of me and wounded two others around us, but I didn't feel so much as shrapnel going by me. Truly, men fell to my right and my left, *but nothing came near me* (Psalm 91:7).

Despite weeks and weeks of off-and-on firefights, we didn't suffer a single KIA throughout the months of June, July, August, or September. I believe that is a direct result of the covering of prayer over me, covering my company as well. Psalm 91 really is a powerful thing that will bring you through. He protects you not only physically, but spiritually as well. Transitioning back to life in the States, being home with my wife, and working with the drastically different garrison, baseline Marine Corps, has really been no problem for me. I credit that to the fact that God protected my mind and soul as well as my body.

I know it is not easy to listen to someone talk about Iraq and give an opinion—especially when it comes from a civilian who hasn't been there, done, seen, or experienced what we have. The word in this book, however, is relevant and real. It is truth. I witnessed miracles from the hand of God, simply by believing and standing on the Word of God in Psalm 91.

Please take it to heart. It will save your life and the lives of others.

Chaplain (Major) Scott Kennedy

I deployed to Kuwait in February of 2003, in support of Operation Iraqi Freedom, where I served as the area support group chaplain. Very shortly after I arrived I was given the responsibility of taking care of the spiritual needs of more than 18,000 coalition troops, supervising more than thirty religious support teams from the U.S. and British military. I coordinated fifteen worship services and twelve Bible studies that took place each week, in two chapel facilities. I pastored the 550-member gospel service and co-pastored the 200-member contemporary service. We had the privilege of baptizing soldiers nearly every week. Another part of my job, as the garrison chaplain, was to brief all the incoming units and the individual replacements.

I always took the opportunity to pray for them and provide them with religious literature. By far the most popular was the Psalm 91 prayer card. I prayed this prayer over thousands of soldiers as they prepared to go into battle. As our unit was called forward into Baghdad, I once again offered up Psalm 91 as our prayer of protection, as our convoy traveled north on the heels of the lead combat unit. Not only did we not sustain any casualties during our tactical movement to the Baghdad International Airport; our entire unit returned home without a scratch.

I was later given the opportunity to lead a group of about forty soldiers and officers to Babylon as the convoy commander. After finishing the safety briefing, my company commander placed a tow bar in one of the Humvees just in case someone broke down. The MPs led us south, out of the city toward Babylon. After about forty-five minutes of traveling, we received a call over the radio saying that one of the Humvees had, in fact, broken down. I had the convoy pull over while I went back to assess the damage.

When I arrived at the site of the crippled jeep, I was presented with good news and bad news. The bad news was that the vehicle had broken down at the most dangerous intersection in all of Iraq. More ambushes happened there than at any other place in the entire country. The good news was that this was the vehicle with the tow bar! I immediately told the guys to shut the hood and hook the Humvee up to mine, and in no time we rejoined the rest of the convoy and were headed for Babylon. We were able to get the vehicle repaired at the base in Babylon and had no problems on our return trip.

As we sat in the debriefing, we learned from the intelligence officer that there had been a deadly ambush just a few hours prior to our passage through that most dangerous intersection. God had rescued us from every trap. He had been our refuge—our place of safety! He had shielded us with His wings, and His faithful promises had been our armor and protection.

Just before I returned to Kuwait in preparation for redeployment, I made a trip to modern-day Mosul, which used to be called Nineveh. The primary purpose of my trip was to visit one of my unit ministry teams, which was supporting the 101st Airborne Division.

But I also sensed there was an even higher purpose. I felt as though this might be a strategic prayer journey into enemy territory.

At that exact time my wife was in Arizona attending a convocation of women leaders, whom Cindy Jacobs had assembled from around the world. Just before I got on the helicopter I was able to speak with my wife, and this group of more than five hundred women went into focused intercession for my prayer journey on the other side of the globe. As I walked around the ruins of Nineveh, I prayed that God would re-dig the wells of revival from Jonah's day. I asked God to bring repentance back to this city, and to expose the hidden things and bring them to light.

After we finished our tour of the ancient city we went into town for a bite to eat. The city seemed very calm and unusually peaceful compared to Baghdad. We met a cute little girl at the restaurant.

I was puzzled when she handed me a crucifix, but after inquiring of the waiter he told me that this girl and her family were Christians. "In fact," he said, "you are in an Assyrian Christian neighborhood!" We were delighted that the Lord had led us into a safe haven. But when we returned to Baghdad Airport we were totally amazed to learn that, not long after we left Mosul, Saddam's sons were killed in a firefight in that very city! God had once again protected us wherever we went. *We did not fear the plague that stalks in darkness or the disaster that strikes at midday.* God had once again been our refuge—our place of safety.

Because of the prayers of the saints back home, and the trust I placed in God, I felt as if I were walking in a bubble of intercession wherever I went. Whether it was in the midst of a mortar attack, or on a convoy;

riding in a helicopter or during a scud alert—I felt God's presence and protection throughout my wartime.

He truly is my place of safety.

Author's Note: Operation PrayerShield is a nonprofit organization that can be viewed at the websites www.prayerforiraq.org and www.operationprayershield. net. Their vision is to raise up an army of intercessors to establish houses of prayer in military communities around the world. Their mission is: (1) to establish a wall of protection around our troops while they are in training exercises and at war; (2) to bless military marriages and families; (3) to intercede and give thanks for our leaders; and (4) to establish the kingdom of God in military communities around the world.

Lt. Carey H. Cash
Author of *A Table in the Presence*

Author's Note: *Lieutenant Carey H. Cash, Chaplain, United States Navy, is a battalion chaplain to infantry Marines. In Operation Iraqi Freedom, his unit* was the first ground combat force to cross the border into Iraq. He is a graduate of The Citadel and Southwestern Baptist Theological Seminary, and was commissioned as a chaplain in 1999. The following excerpts come from Lt. Cash's book, A Table in the Presence. These are the stories of the men with whom he was privileged to serve.

You could never talk Staff Sergeant Bryan Jackway out of Psalm 91. The words of that psalm had carried him through Desert Storm in 1991, and through the bloody streets of Somalia. Its promises had been his strength just days ago when enemy mortars had nearly taken his life at the Saddam Canal: "A thousand may fall at your side and ten thousand at your right hand, but it shall not approach you…for you have made the LORD, my refuge, even the Most High, your dwelling place" (Psalm 91:7, 9).

That was the very moment when every man in Jackway's vehicle should have been killed. Without warning, from point-blank range, an RPG struck the driver's-side doorframe, twelve inches from where the driver was sitting. It sent waves of fire and shrapnel rippling through the cramped compartment. It was the kind of direct hit that often leaves no human remains.

In short, a high-explosive rocket exploded with all of its force inside the cabin of an armored Humvee, manned by four men. And yet, as the rocket struck the doorframe it was as if an unseen hand channeled its force. Most of the explosion passed through the driver's open window, while the rest of it smashed against the inside of the front glass.

The windshield exploded from the inside out. In a millisecond of deafening sound, the thick, bulletproof-glass windshield disintegrated into a fireball. Thousands of jagged shards showered the paved road in front of Jackway's still-moving Humvee, like a deadly rainstorm. All four men were engulfed in a scorching wall of heat and flames. Marines driving behind Jackway's Humvee saw the hit. They knew beyond a doubt that America had just lost four boys.

Opening his eyes after the blinding flash, Jackway grabbed his chest and arm. He kept pounding and squeezing to make sure he was still there. "Dear God— I'm alive!" he shouted. Jackway immediately picked up his radio and started calling in casualties. He didn't bother to look at them. He knew very well that no one could have emerged from such an explosion alive, much less unscathed.

But as he glanced beside and behind him, there sat the others, alive and uninjured. Jackway began frisking the body of his driver. He knew that it's not uncommon for men who are mortally wounded in battle to not realize for a few seconds, or even minutes, that they've been hit or are dying. The driver had been sitting precisely where the blast had occurred.

"I started running my hands down his back, on his legs, up his neck, patting him down, looking for an entry wound, an exit wound where shrapnel had hit," Jackway said. "But there was nothing. I couldn't believe what I was seeing."

Jackway couldn't seem to get the words of a psalm out of his head—a Scripture he had read many times in preparation for going off to war. His heart leaped as he experienced its newfound power and meaning as never before.

> I will set him securely on high,
> because he has known My name.
> He will call upon Me, and I will
> answer him; I will be with him in
> trouble; I will rescue him and honor
> him. With a long life I will satisfy
> him and let him see My salvation.
> (Psalm 91:14–16)

God has unique ways of demonstrating the importance of His Word to men who need that extra *faith booster*. Corporal Hardy, who always kept his fellow passengers busy with frequent references and quotations to and from the Bible, had a green pocket Bible that had become something of a spiritual symbol in the cabin. Once it was taken in the Humvee and passed around from man to man to read silently or aloud during one of the storms that was so intense, with the sand in the air so thick that it was actually blocking some of the radio frequencies.

Hardy had pried open the Humvee's door and stepped into the storm, forgetting that the Bible had been lying in his lap Later he realized that the green Bible, which he and his three buddies had come to depend upon as a sign of God's presence, was lost in the sand. The final hours of the storm were unquestionably the worst. Seventy-mile-per-hour gusts of wind drove not only sand but rain, and then golf-ball-sized hail, screaming at the convoy sideways like a meteor shower. When the wind was finally reduced to a gentle breeze, Corporals Dickens, Hardy, Batke, and Beavers—along with the rest of the convoy—received immediate instructions to refuel and push out.

The road where Dickens's vehicle had sat idling all night came alive, as dozens of Humvees, trucks, and artillery pieces churned and dug through the sea of red muck that the rain had produced. After refueling, Hardy got back into line and was making his way back to the convoy's original lineup. Then, without warning, Hardy slammed on his brakes. "Sir, it's—it's the Bible!"

Suddenly, a string of vehicles behind him had to slam on their brakes as Hardy opened his door and jumped out. He was smiling from ear to ear, holding in his hand the lost Bible that had disappeared the night before, right in the middle of the storm. And the strangest thing of all was its perfect condition.

The Bible had been dropped from the vehicle onto a dirt road, and had then been assaulted for hours by seventy-mile-per-hour winds carrying stinging sand, rain, and hail. It had been lying on a road that, for the past two hours, had borne the weight of every vehicle in the convoy. Still, the Bible had not moved an inch from where it had first landed. And it was not torn. It wasn't bent. It wasn't even wet.

"Sir, this is a sign from God!" said Hardy, clutching it to his chest.

~

Some things you will never know—well, at least not on this side. Corporal Zebulon Batke, M-19 grenade launcher, said, "It got so bad, I could literally feel the bullets whizzing by me. I was going to get hit at any moment. I could see the shadowy outlines of men running all around me, above me on rooftops, everywhere. But something just kept me going.

"Then came the heart-stopper. Something told me to look to my right, and when I did I could see the silhouette of a man who couldn't have been more than twenty-five feet away. He was kneeling with an RPG, and it was pointed right at me."

What happened next was simply unexplainable. Before Batke could whirl his M-19 around and start shooting, the man—for no good reason—stood up as if he'd seen a ghost. He looked at another gunman standing close by, waved his arms frantically, and together the two ran full speed into a darkened alleyway.

They never once looked back. The enemy gunman had had every opportunity to launch his RPG into the stopped Humvee. Yet instead of taking the point-blank shot, he simply ran. Yelling something to his cohort in Arabic, the two fled for their lives.

What on earth had the man seen? What caused him not to shoot his missile? Why did he turn and run?

When they finally drove through the iron gates of the presidential palace, Captain Will Dickens, headquarters company commander, recalled having an overwhelming desire to fall to his knees and thank God. Tears of emotion and gratitude streamed from many of the men's eyes. Corporal Hardy just kept smiling and pointing to the worn leathery green Bible that still sat unmoved on the radio mount. "I knew it! I knew it when we found it in the storm. God was going to protect us."

Corporal Ayani Dawson had been baptized as a new Christian just weeks earlier. Now he grinned. "Chaplain, remember those angels, the ones your wife talked about—the legions? They were surrounding us. I should be dead, Chaplain, but God was with me."

> For He will give His angels charge
> concerning you, to guard you in all
> your ways (Psalm 91:11).

⌒

Early on April 12, as I made my way around Saddam's palace grounds, I felt compelled to keep talking to the men and listening to their stories. I sensed in them a deep need, even a compulsion, to articulate their wonder and amazement at what God had brought them through. And this wasn't true of only a handful of Marines. From the youngest private to the oldest veteran, every man had a story to tell.

Their stories seemed to have one common thread—they all believed they had been in the midst of a modern-day miracle. As they told me what they had seen, their eyes lit up and their faces glowed. It was clear to me that I wasn't merely in the company of warriors, but of witnesses.

As they spoke, with tears in their eyes and bullet holes through their clothes, I realized that I, too, was a witness. These were not men who had "found religion" momentarily, or who were courteously acknowledging the practical aspects of prayer or faith in times of need. These were men who had stumbled onto something historic, a story that had to be told.

Captain Nick Catechis, Army
Army Transport Unit Miracle, Iraq

by Kay Gibson, cofounder, Houston
Marine Moms

About a year ago I met this Army mom, Judith Cook, who was helping her son's unit—the 15th Transportation Unit from Fort Sill, Oklahoma—get ready to deploy to Iraq three days after Christmas 2004. Judith's son, Nick Catechis, is a captain of the Army Transport Unit, with 150 soldiers in it. The commander's wife contacted Judith and told her this group delivers supplies on the road between the Baghdad Airport and Abu Ghraib, so they were expecting extremely high casualties. She was wondering if Judith would start making a quilted banner with a gold star in memory of each soldier they expected to be killed in action or severely injured.

When Judith asked what sort of casualty rate they were expecting, she was told it could be from 50 to 75 percent. Judith then found on the Internet some camouflage bandanas with the Ninety-first Psalm printed on them, which is considered the *Psalm of Protection* for our troops. Judith hand-delivered these bandanas to the soldiers in the unit and made them promise to say the psalm every day before their missions. Every day both the officers and soldiers would say this psalm together.

During the deployment Nick's unit was attacked on an almost daily basis with IEDs and mortars, and by snipers, yet there were countless stories of mortars that never detonated; mortars that exploded nearby but caused no shrapnel injuries to Nick's group;

ambushes on their Humvees yet no injuries. In fact, I have a picture of a bullet hole through the window of Nick's Humvee. It missed him, his driver, and the mortar man by an inch.

Author's note: *The following was submitted by Judith Cook*

In another incident, several of Nick's men were in the mess hall when a mortar exploded less than twenty feet away. Shrapnel landed all around, yet none of the soldiers was injured. There was also an attack on the Army buildings in which the soldiers sleep, and three of the buildings were damaged, but the mortar that landed on top of Nick's building was a dud. Several of Nick's men were in a PX near Baghdad when it was attacked. Everyone in the PX was injured, except Nick's men. On July 23, 2005, I received the following email from Nick:

"We got hit again really bad night before last, in three separate engagements. We received small arms fire on the first two, and another explosive on the third. I've attached a photo of the vehicle that took most of the blast. Remarkably, other than a possible concussion and some ringing ears, no one was hurt seriously. This armor we have is really good stuff.

Unfortunately, we've had the chance to try it out on more than one occasion, but at least we know it is good stuff.

"We also had a mortar attack on the same day. One of the guys was outside working and heard a really loud noise and had rocks thrown on him. He looked over and saw an unexploded mortar lying on the gravel about ten feet from him. Needless to say, he took off running. If you are praying for us, it must be working. That's the only explanation of how no one has been seriously injured yet."

Day after day these soldiers gathered to pray this psalm together. On December, 2005, after almost a year in Iraq, Nick and his unit returned home—all 150 soldiers. They did not lose one soldier, nor were any of them injured. The power of prayer is awesome!

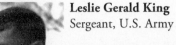

Leslie Gerald King
Sergeant, U.S. Army

Author's Note: *Seadrift, Texas, has quite a history of standing on the promises of Psalm 91 and having their soldiers come back safely home to them. This is the next generation's story, from the grandson of WWII veteran Gerald McCown. This is truly how Psalm 91 has affected the next generation of soldiers.*

During the entire first year of my deployment to Iraq, there was a very tangible sense of the protective covering of God's hand. We had not lost a single soldier—no one in the company had been hurt, in fact; not anyone I knew in any personal way had ever been harmed. I felt that same protective covering for everyone I saw.

Emotionally, I felt no loss of life impact that usually results from war. At twenty-three, as a young man off to war, I was expecting some action. However, I did not see a single person killed, nor did I ever see a dead body! I experienced none of the gruesomeness of war during the time I served, even though it was really prevalent in the Iraqi conflict. The prayer covering of the church and my family gave me a totally different battle experience. It wasn't because we hadn't seen danger, because we had, but there was a pervading sense of security over us and everyone that we knew on the battlefield. We had been through "rough stuff" without a scratch and had felt protected and peaceful the whole time!

So dramatic was this to me, and so real, that there

were times when I would see one of my buddies in danger and I would go stand in front of him. The protection was so real to me it was almost as if I could reach out and touch it.

However, in April, there was talk of our returning home, and something changed. It felt as though the prayer cover was lifting. I could sense danger I had never felt before for those around me. Personally, I felt okay, but I was aware of the danger for the people around me and, all at once, everything began flaring up. Within days of my realizing that something was wrong we began losing soldiers in my company, we ran out of supplies, and our time was extended for another four months because of the flare-ups. There was a drastic cut in our water and food rations. What I experienced during those couple of weeks, I knew shouldn't be happening because I had a promise! My family and church were praying Psalm 91 over me and the others in my company.

The moment we got to a location where I could make calls home, I started calling the churches that were committed to praying for us. When I called my aunt and uncle, they found that the bulletin board displaying our pictures, as a reminder to pray for us, had been taken down. Relief had swept over the people when some of the soldiers had returned home and the news had reported that an end was in sight; therefore, prayers had let up.

When I asked the date that the bulletin board had come down, it matched up with the time when I sensed in Iraq that something had gone wrong with our prayer covering. After hearing about the flare-ups we were having, the church immediately put our pictures back up and started fervently praying again. The results were immediate. The difference was uncanny and the protection once again was tangible. From that moment on, not one more soldier in our company was lost.

All this has testified to me firsthand of what it means when people pray. From our first station in Germany we were all shipped in different directions, yet every one of us made it back without anyone from this German church fellowship being harmed. Even though we went to fight in all different places—everywhere from Iraq to Kuwait—the prayer covering went with us. I am a believer who knows for certain that soldiers tangibly experience the difference when people pray over them!

Col James E. Agnew

Psalm 91 and the Chemical Platoon

While I served as the First Cavalry Division Support Command Chaplain during Operation Desert Storm, my troop coverage responsibility included the Division Chemical Platoon. Prior to the beginning of the ground war, my mission included visiting all the troopers preparing to move forward. At that time there was a tremendous concern that Iraq would deploy chemical weapons once we crossed the border. The Chemical Platoon's mission required them to go ahead of the main body to determine if chemical weapons had been deployed, and what type. Needless to say, being forward on the battle field presented numerous challenges and an increased risk of contact, ambush, mine fields, and chemical contamination. These soldiers were well aware of the risks and skillfully trained to deal with whatever obstacle they might encounter.

As I paid the Chemical Platoon an early visit one morning, I noticed they had already gathered into a circle around the Platoon Leader. I thought to myself, "This is great; I'll have a captive audience of the entire platoon already waiting for me."

As I got closer, I noticed they had Bibles in their hands and they were about to have their daily devotional as a platoon. They were thrilled to see me and asked if I would read the 91st Psalm and pray for them. Apparently, they had started the morning formations by reading the 91st Psalm and prayer ever since they arrived in Saudi. As the alert to move out that day had been given, the soldiers felt that the Lord had sent me at just the right time to speak peace to their hearts and encourage their faith just before they embarked on the most dangerous mission they had ever faced.

As I began to read the Psalm 91 I sensed the strong presence of the Lord among us. The anxious looks on the troopers' faces gave way to a calm, peaceful confidence. That blessed assurance enabled that platoon to complete its mission with an unwavering faith that God was with them, and the promises of Psalm 91 were personally for them. The Chemical Platoon accomplished its mission without a single casualty. I knew in my heart that the Lord directed me to this "divine appointment" that brought His presence and peace to some anxious troopers, enabling them to walk by faith and serve God and Country with great success.

CH (LTC) Dixey Behnken
Task Force Adler Chaplain

Over thirty-eight hundred troops came to our Task Force Adler, a large brigade consisting of two battalions from Darmstadt, Germany, four battalions from Kitzingen, Germany, and four battalions from the States—Fort Hood, Texas, and Fort Lewis, Washington. Our units settled into many locations across Iraq, but our headquarters became Camp Victory, Baghdad.

Our testimony is that every troop who came to Iraq returned. Yes, there were some injuries from IEDs, VBIEDs, mortars, and rockets, but not one soldier lost his life. Not one soldier lost a limb, eyesight, or hearing.

Brigadier General Dennis Via, commander of 5th Signal Command, stated at the Uncasing of the Colors Celebration that this feat was nothing less than a miracle. We chaplains also believe it to be a miracle, for which we and all the soldiers' families are thankful. Over three hundred combat convoy missions were made in the disbursal, maintenance, and replacement of signal equipment, including over five hundred successful helicopter flight missions. Task Force Adler provided the communications for coalition forces over the land mass of Iraq, covering more than 140,000 square miles.

Prior to our departure hundreds of our soldiers and family members were kneeling on the streets in front of the command headquarters, joining my wife, Julianne, and me as I led them in a prayer for safe deployment. For many of us, this was our first deployment and we did not quite know what to expect. God heard our prayers and rewarded the requests of our hearts.

Michael Payne, Winchester, Virginia
Freelance writer; five times to Iraq
www.takeastandministries.org

In 1998 at the age of forty-eight, I was constantly dogged by hopelessness and despair that would not leave—and with the realization that I was never going to smile from within again. I had spent thirty-three of those forty-eight years drinking, drugging, gambling, and committing multiple adulteries in vain attempts to grab temporary moments of what I thought would bring happiness.

These things no longer brought any satisfaction, and no respite from the depression and thoughts of suicide and other symptoms attributed to PTSD that were now hounding me constantly. My second marriage was falling apart and my two sons from my first marriage could no longer stand to be around me. My second wife, in a marriage that had always been volatile, was demanding that I move out. The futility of my sinful life brought the realization that I could not go back into the sex, drugs, and rock-and-roll lifestyle that was now leading me, quickly, toward death through suicide. But the Lord had other plans for my life.

In the fall of 1998 a Christian from Guatemala, seeing the pain and distress in my face, said to me, "Brother Michael, I read Psalm 91 every day before I come to work!" He did not elaborate but the Spirit of the Lord was at work and He gave me ears to hear. I started reading Psalm 91 the next morning and continued doing so every morning after that—and sometimes several times a day.

Eventually, the time came when, as I would read it, not only did a smile come to my face, but more important, a smile came into my heart. I knew that the Lord was speaking directly to me, and that He was keeping all His promises in Psalm 91. There is not one part of Psalm 91 that I did not grab hold of and believe, as a covering for every aspect of the battle in my life. It not only saved my life, but the psalm led me to believe in God and, one year later, to give my life to Jesus.

I still carry in my wallet a handwritten copy of Psalm 91 that was given to me by a dear friend. It often reminded me of the power of God's Word as I traveled through Iraq, Afghanistan, and even right here in the United States. I have been to Iraq as a freelance Christian radio reporter four different times, embedded alongside the U.S. Armed Forces. I know that the Lord has saved my life on several specific occasions, and many times when I was not even aware. God is sovereign over every bullet and every piece of shrapnel that flies. He gives me victory when all would look like defeat. If we but stand in the shadow of the Almighty, He will deliver us without fail. He has given me peace beyond understanding in all circumstances.

I am set free of alcohol, drugs, sexual sin, gambling, and worldly ways. I am not recovering from any of these; I am set free. I am a new creation in the name of Jesus! I am one of the slaves given freedom through Jesus and His truth. I owe it all to God and to the truth, the way, and the life expressed in Psalm 91, and in Jesus Christ.

Mike DiSanza, NYPD
President and founding officer
of Cops for Christ International

Author's note: Mike gave us this testimony in his own words. His story gave me chills when I heard him telling it in his strong New York accent. I was moved by Mike's humor but could feel an undercurrent of urgency in him. Mike gave me one clear message to get out: "Too much of our time is spent worrying about things that don't matter, like our green lawn having a brown spot. If we don't get the gospel out, people are going to hell! One day we will wake up in forever. And it is a forever hell." Mike shared over the phone the dramatic testimony of his unusual introduction to Christ and his wife's reluctant conversion. I encourage you to get his book and share it with a friend, because his testimony was every bit as dramatic as the Psalm 91 story of protection. Now, here's Mike's story in his own words.

Over my system came the message: 72nd Street and Broadway—Manhattan! I knew the meaning of the code: cop in trouble and needs assistance. I rushed to the subway and found a crowd of people around the cop, and they refused to let him get his prisoner. I walked directly over and cuffed the prisoner. The crowd went wild.

One man shouted, "Here comes the train!" Let's throw the cop in the subway!" The crowd converted into a mob. I felt myself moving toward the subway track, being pushed by this angry crowd of people who were intending to hurl me onto the tracks in front of the speeding train. I could hear the sound and see the lights of the train coming out from the tunnel. I was being pushed toward the pit.

Being a new Christian, I cried out the best prayer I knew, "Jesus help!" Suddenly, two big black guys got up and started pushing the crowd. They parted the crowd and got over to me and said, "Follow us!" I grabbed the prisoner and followed as they parted the mob, and felt the other cop right on my heels hanging onto my jacket. The two men ushered us back to the patrol car and I loaded the prisoner in the back seat. He was still screaming his mouth off about how he hated cops. I turned around to thank the two strangers and was surprised that neither of them was there. *Oh, well,* I thought, and muttered my thanks to them anyway.

I jumped in and the other cop got in next to the driver. He thanked me gratefully for my help. I deflected the compliment and said to him, "Thank God for those two big black guys pushing the crowd apart, telling us to follow them and moving us to the car!"

He said, "I didn't hear nothing! I didn't see nothing! And I never heard anyone tell us to follow them!" Still puzzled, I asked, "Eddie, how could you NOT see them? You were right behind us!"

When I turned around, I read this message in 3-D through the windshield: *Angels are ministering spirits to help those who will believe.* (See Hebrews 1:4.) At that moment I realized what had happened and said to myself, "My gosh, those guys were angels!" God really does give His angels charge concerning us (Psalm 91:11).

To order Mike's book, *A Cop for Christ,* write to him at Mike DiSanza Ministries, 3231 S. Eagle Point, Inverness, FL 34450. Or visit www.acopforchrist.com.

Carlos Aviles Jr.
New York Police Department

Author's Note: *Carlos Aviles Jr., who retired as a detective in the NYPD Special Victims (sex crimes) Unit in the Bronx, serves as president of "Police Officers for Christ," a recognized fraternal organization of New York City Police Department. The Chief of Staff of the New York mayor's office called Carlos to work Ground Zero. That turned into a seven-month ministry, and with the help of churches and the use of an abandoned Catholic Church, Carlos fed firemen and cops around the clock and distributed Bibles to them. Until then, Carlos was called a holy roller and took a lot of ribbing and ridicule. When he would ask to pray for them at roll call before they went out on patrol, cops would pipe up with "Hurry up!" His half-box of Bibles was seldom used. But through the crisis of 9/11, New York saw the love of God and His hands working through believers. It was a remarkable change—everyone stood up for prayer at roll call, and Carlos couldn't keep up with the demand for Bibles. The following story was written by Peggy Joyce Ruth, based on interviews with Carlos Aviles.*

Law enforcement officers, like our military personnel, put themselves in harm's way every single day they are on duty. According to current U.S. Department of Justice statistics, assailants using handguns, rifles, or shotguns killed 594 law enforcement officers from 1992 to 2001, an average of more than one violent death a week each year. Who, more than they, need the protection of our Psalm 91 covenant?

In the United States, 665,555 full-time officers are employed by almost 14,000 city, college, county, and state police agencies. As a group they suffer from abnormally high divorce, alcoholism, suicide, and mortality rates. The average age of death for police officers is sixty-six, according to a forty-year study conducted at Rochester (New York) Institute of Technology.

When I called Carlos to tell him that I had seen his interview in *Charisma*[12] magazine from a few years back, I asked him to tell me his story in his own words. I could tell that Psalm 91 had special meaning to him. Working in the Bronx, working homicide, working Special Victims (sex crimes) for years with the NYPD, working with other cops…I knew he had stories that begged to be told.

The first thing Carlos told me was his very personal recap of the Ninety-first Psalm. He said it was the psalmist telling God how wonderful He is, how much he can be trusted, how there is a safe place under His wings, and how He deserves to be worshiped. Then in verse 14, God interrupts the psalmist and says, "Yes, and this is what I will do for you because you love Me," much like a man does when his son calls him on the phone—he cuts in to tell that son how much he means to him. "In the same way," Carlos explained, "this psalm is very applicable to police officers—when officers pray, God will respond to them in a personal way."

Carlos confirmed the high statistics of divorce and alcoholism among cops and explained the reason for it. The "bottom cop" or "rookie" has the worst jobs and sees the worst part of society. "That rookie cop is the one who at the scene of an accident has to count the pieces of a child and the whole time he is thinking, 'I have a two-year-old at home.'

"And the cop keeps this all inside," Carlos went on, "and puts up a front to survive, but the only way he will truly make it is by turning to the Lord. The cop has to have a personal relationship with God to survive the pressures of the job. The psalmist saw thousands of people falling around him, but God was faithful to him."

Carlos spoke as a man who had experience with the faithfulness of God. "God will respond to you personally when you respond to Him."

Carlos has a firsthand story from his police work of the power of Psalm 91. One night the other men on duty had teamed up and he was odd man out, so to keep from losing a day's work he took a duty post without a partner, which is known as a foot-post assignment. With his hat under his arm so he would not be easily identified, Carlos was watching up and down the neighborhood, keeping his back against the wall for protection. Suddenly he saw a man leaving a club with a Macy's shopping bag in his hands.

Carlos identified himself as an officer and pulled his gun to make the arrest. As he expected, the man hadn't been on a late night shopping excursion—the bag was filled with several pounds of marijuana.

Expecting defiant resistance, Carlos was somewhat puzzled when the offered none, dropped the bag, put his hands behind his back and waited for handcuffs. *This is the easiest arrest I have ever made,* Carlos thought, and he called for backup.

In booking, when the desk sergeant asked Carlos, "Who was with you on the arrest?" Carlos stated, "I was alone on the arrest!" The perpetrator overheard his report and started shouting, "You're lying! You're lying! There was like ten of them! I was going to make a run, but all those cops with guns were all around me!" Carlos thought the guy was *off the wall*.

But as he went back to his car, Carlos remembered the ease of the arrest and the subdued actions of the man, and then he remembered the promise of the Ninety-first Psalm. It became quite apparent to Carlos that the man was seeing the angels that encamp around us. Citing Psalm 91:11, he added: "That's why I know God does give His angels charge over us."

LT. Chaplain Terry Sponholz
President, Firefighters for Christ,
Citrus County Florida

We had finished a Code Two run to the hospital (heart attack) when we received another emergency call from my captain: "Our baby has quit breathing!" You could hear the commotion in the background. His wife was in a panic, and administrating breaths to their two-week-old daughter brought no response. The couple was hysterical.

The driver of our fire engine made record time with the pedal all the way to the metal. It was a seven- or eight-mile drive from the hospital to their home. How long had their baby been without oxygen to the brain? Had damage already taken place? We beat the ambulance to the scene.

It is a moment that stands still forever in your mind when a non-breathing, two-week-old baby that is limp, blue in the face and lips, lifeless, and with arms and legs flopping is thrown into your arms by your captain. The captain had only one direction for me.

"You pray a lot! Do what you do, please!"

And that is when the Holy Spirit fell on me. I cried out to the Lord and started praying in tongues. This Catholic family had thrown their baby into the hands of a Pentecostal chaplain! But when the Holy Spirit fell, the power went into that baby in my arms. And that baby came back to life, without my ever putting on the mask or turning on the oxygen.

By the time the ambulance arrived the child was

totally back to normal. The Holy Spirit had blown life into that child all over again. Fear had gripped the parents, not only because of the baby's being without oxygen for more than the four-minute limit, but because it was compounded with the pain they felt from when the captain's nephew had drowned.

"It wasn't God's fault that Tommy (the nephew) had died," I had told them, but it had left a *mean* feeling inside of the captain's body. That day the pain had compounded in his heart. He had expressed the only way he knew to express it: "Do what you do!"

And those words, spoken in faith toward God, brought a miracle to his child that day!

> He will call upon Me, and I will
> answer Him, I will be with him
> in trouble and I will rescue him!
> (Psalm 91:15)

John Johnson
Texas Youth Commission
Special Tactics and Response Team

As a former leader of the Special Tactics and Response team at our local Texas Youth Commission juvenile correctional facility, I was at times called upon to travel across the state to other facilities that were having problems. Our duty was to restore and maintain safe operations in struggling facilities. This is usually a risky adventure, since we are required to control violent behavior of incarcerated juveniles without the use of guns. Tension is usually high between staff and the youth we are charged to control.

Before I started going on these trips I had been learning from Peggy Joyce's Psalms 91 books about the special covenant of protection God provides. God's Word works, and I learned to apply these biblical truths to my work assignments. I knew the risks going into these tense situations, and I prepared my response teams through physical training, proper equipping, and most important, by praying His protection over me and each of my team members.

Every time we traveled God blessed me and each of my team members by protecting us physically and in every other way. At each facility where we were sent, we were always outnumbered by the youth. However, every time, just as Psalms 91 says, they would fall at our side.

One incident in particular stands out. I regularly would train our STAR team to control riot situations. On this particular trip we definitely had to put this

252

training to work. One dorm of youth overpowered staff and took control of the unit, tearing it up severely. The guys went crazy and ripped a water fountain from the wall, completely destroyed the washer and dryer, and threw a TV through a glass window. It was not a pretty sight.

We were charged to take it back and we went in quoting Scripture and fighting the battle spiritually. It took less than sixty minutes. We faced heavy objects being thrown at us and other dangerous, homemade weapons that had been fashioned to harm us. We were not afraid of any of those arrows flying against us. Some of the youth were injured, but not one staff member was hurt. Let me repeat that: Not one staff member was hurt!

I had prayed this psalm of protection over us, and praise God, we were able to take control of the unit without being harmed. I was determined not to let the enemy hurt my staff or let him cause any more destruction now that Jesus was in the house, but I am still amazed as I think of what God did for us. It felt like His shield went before us, and I came out with not even one scratch or bruise!

After peace had been restored we walked through the dorm and I recovered a twelve-inch homemade knife, made of razor-sharp half-inch-thick glass taken from a shattered television, among other dangerous objects. These weapons could have easily killed one of our staff. With God's protection, that did not (and could not) happen.

Our superintendent, a godly man of faith, would also send us out under a covering of prayer. Every time, we brought home every man and woman from our team, safe and sound. God not only protected us but He also honored our efforts. Based on our actions to provide STAR team help to our sister facilities who were in need, my STAR team earned the 2005 Institutional Team award from the TYC Executive Director.

We cheated, however, by using an extra piece of gear—our Psalm 91 shield.

Hudson Plane Crash Miracle

Andrew Gray had recently returned from his second tour of duty in Afghanistan—one of those long, fifteen-month stints. He had served twelve months in Afghanistan before that, with a one-year break between the two tours. During each one his mother had spent many hours praying Psalm 91 protection over him on a daily basis.

Once he got home, Andrew decided to celebrate with a trip to New York for the birthday of his fiancée, Stephanie. Literally, just a few minutes after Andrew and Stephanie got airborne on their return flight from New York City, Andrew called his dad to say that their plane had just gone down in the Hudson River.

"Turn on the TV, dad!" was all he had time to say. At that very moment, the local TV station interrupted its regular programming with a breaking news story about Flight 1549, which had just crashed into the Hudson River.

Andrew's parents stared incredulously at the footage of this airplane floating in the water. The right wing was listing, but all the passengers who had been on the wings were being picked up by ferries. Andrew had called from the wing of that plane.

His parents watched and waited to hear from Andrew again. When his next call finally came through, Andrew told his parents that he and Stephanie had been on the right wing of the plane, even as it had begun to sink. They had stepped out in frigid water up to their ankles, but soon the water rose above their knees. They were being pushed farther and farther from the fuselage toward the tip of the wing, as more passengers came out the emergency door. As ferries came to the rescue, Andrew and Stephanie leaped from the wing to a ladder hanging down from one of them.

Later, Andrew said he knew there was something wrong with the airplane when he heard a loud pop and then saw black smoke coming from the engine. As the plane banked to make a turn, Andrew reassured Stephanie that it would be all right. They weren't far from the airport and the plane was returning to land. But as they looked out the window, Andrew felt a strange silence. Usually you can hear the hum of the engines, but he couldn't hear any engine at all. They were gliding, and when they started losing altitude fast he knew they were in trouble.

At that moment the pilot came over the intercom and told the passengers to brace for impact. Andrew knew they would be going down in the water, which somewhat relieved him. He thought that might give them a better chance for survival, and that brought a spark of hope mingled with fear.

He remembered telling Stephanie that, when they crashed, they would need to get off of the plane in a hurry. They kissed each other, said "I love you," huddled close to one another, and began praying together as they braced for the impact. Andrew said he had all kinds of scenarios running through his head in that one long minute before the impact. What if the plane tore apart and they got sucked down into the water? He knew hypothermia could take over and their lungs could freeze quickly, along with their extremities. He said that he thought about the fact that he'd made it through two deployments to Afghanistan, and now it was all going to end like this!

Or was it? By the grace of God, and because of the experience of a very skilled pilot, the airplane made a miraculous landing on the water, followed by a surprisingly calm disembarkment. Once they'd been rescued the passengers were taken to three different terminals, so it took a while before the airline knew that all the passengers were accounted for, with no loss of life.

When Andrew and Stephanie arrived by train at their home, their friends and families praised God and marveled at the miracle He'd brought about. God had been all over that flight—placing Chesley Sullenberger at the helm of the plane, keeping the often busy Hudson waterway clear of ferries, barges, and boats, keeping the plane in one piece and afloat long enough for all 155 passengers to be rescued, firmly planting their almost frozen feet on a slippery surface in a swift current and not allowing them to fall.

Witnessing and experiencing this miracle firsthand certainly strengthened and affirmed Andrew's existing faith. It was obvious that the protective power of Psalm 91, which had been prayed over Andrew while he was deployed in Afghanistan, continued to cover him. Captain Sullenberger is a gifted pilot, but he would be the first to admit that he was just the co-pilot that day. The real Pilot, God Himself, took control of that flight.

Gratitude to Our Military

Lieutenant Carey Cash addressed a difficult and painful question on page 240 of his book *A Table in the Presence*: What about those who are dying almost daily? Where was God's supernatural protection for them? He answers this question with a contrast between the protection on the life of Daniel and the martyr death of Stephen. He contrasted the scriptural difference of both men of God—Daniel's outcome (lion's den intervention and protection) and Stephen's outcome (laying down one's life out of love).

Lieutenant Cash pointed out how two men side by side can have different encounters. Similarly, I would like to address Scriptures which are also often found side by side, but which allude to two different outcomes. How can the Bible promise protection and healing, and at the same time (often in the same passage) promise rewards for a Christian martyr's death?

Luke 21:18 gives us a promise that not a hair of our head will perish. This is a great protection verse—right down to *hair protection*! This promises that in the midst of very intense conflict we can walk out with not one trace of injury. Yet two verses before in Luke 21:16, it says some will be betrayed, and some will be put to death, because of the name of Jesus. This passage speaks of the horrors men can do to one another via deceit, disloyalty, and betrayal.

Similarly, Hebrews 11 is the great Hall of the Champions of Faith who escaped, overcame, and were protected. Verse by verse, story by story, it documents those who prevailed by their faith. Verses 32 through the first part of verse 35 declare that there are so many stories of protection, deliverance, escape, and even resurrection from the dead they can't all be told in one setting. However, in the last half of verse 35 it says that some "did not accept their release" and experienced torture, chains, imprisonment. Here again, amid the countless testimonies of protection, we find a reference to those who apparently chose to sacrifice their lives.

We have the contrasting experiences of James and Peter. In Acts, the church prayed fervently for Peter's release and Peter had a supernatural deliverance from a sure martyr's death, when an angel came and led him out of prison (Acts 12:5). However, we observe in verse 2 that the church had the despair of losing James, an event which stirred them to much prayer for Peter's deliverance. Again, we see other people's choice to pray for a situation can dramatically change the outcome.

So, how does one decide which verse applies? Each of these verses references the choices men make. Dietrich Bonhoeffer (1906–1945) is said to have wrestled with this same question when, as a pastor, he was confronted with the choice of being a part of an assassination attempt on the life of Adolf Hitler. He is reported to have chosen to do what he could to restrain evil by assisting with the scheme. But again, the inward conflict surfaced in Bonhoeffer when a young man came to him, wanting prayer before he delivered the bomb; and Bonhoeffer knew the young man would be killed in the process. After deliberation, Bonhoeffer prayed this verse: "Greater love has no man when he lays down his lives for his friends." He knew the man had chosen to use his life to set other men free.

During the times when our children have been involved in proclaiming Christ in hostile countries, they have sometimes made the proclamation, "This is not the time I will lay down my head on this mission field! There may come a time we sign our testimony in our own blood, but I choose to find the way of escape out of this situation" (based on 1 Corinthians 10:13). God has dramatically delivered them out of many close calls, and they have experienced supernatural protection in very unpredictable circumstances.

In the timing of the sacrificial death of Jesus, you also see the choice element involved. Countless times men sought to kill Christ, but He walked through the midst of them. However, at the time of His trial He made it very clear that His life would not be literally "taken" from Him—that He, instead, was laying it down on His own initiative (John 10:18). Yet, Jesus acknowledged clearly the enormous shield around Him in Matthew 26:53, when He said that He could appeal to His Father for twelve legions of angels for protection. That is some firepower when you consider how many men one angel killed in the Old Testament. This passage in Matthew 26 has been called the *prayer never prayed,* for Jesus made the choice not to utilize his arsenal of protection.

A soldier has made a choice to defend his country's freedom with his life. Jesus acknowledged this need to defend earthly kingdoms against violent men and stated that, if He had an earthly kingdom, His men would fight to defend Him (John 18:36). As free individuals we are greatly indebted to those who have fought to keep us free, and we are deeply grateful to those who have laid down their lives to protect the families back home. Many brave men and women have heroically given their lives for the sake of restraining evil, and there are no words to adequately express our gratitude and indebtedness.

The hope of this book, however, is that many military personnel will see that God has given protection promises for those who will accept them, so that as few as possible deaths will need to occur. We must remember that the ultimate sacrifice was Jesus, who died in the place of every man. But it required only *one* sacrifice to buy our eternal freedom, and Jesus has already paid for that with His own death.

I pray that God-fearing men and women, and their families, will continue to pray for God's shield of protection around those who defend this country so they will be delivered out of harm's way!

Daniel Clay

Author's Note: *Daniel Clay's letter, reproduced below exactly as he wrote it, expresses so well the love and devotion that he and so many others have felt for their country. I want to extend my appreciation to Daniel's father for sharing his letter with the president, and thus with the world.*

An interesting additional note. *A friend, Joyce Dulin, gave me two numbers: one a White House number for finding Daniel Clay's father and the other a number for Bill Bunce to substantiate another entirely different matter. With the names and numbers on the paper in front of me, still I "accidentally" reversed them and found the White House had no way of contacting the Clays while the unrelated number led me right to the Clay's private line. After months of futile searching on our own, only God could have had me reverse the numbers when I had all the information written on a paper in front of me. Later, as I saw Daniel's picture and opened his letter, I knew why the search had been so important; words will never be enough to say thank you for the heroic sacrifices for our freedom.*

December 7, 2005

President George Bush
The White House
1600 Pennsylvania Ave. NW
Washington, DC 20500

Dear President Bush,

My name is Bud Clay. My son, SSgt Daniel Clay - USMC was killed last week 12/01/05 in Iraq. He was one of the ten Marines killed by the IED in Fallujah.

Dan was a Christian – he knew Jesus as Lord and Savior – so we know where he is. In his final letter (one left with me for the family - to be read in case of his death) he says "if you are reading this, it means my race is over." He's home now – his and our real home.

I am writing to you – to tell you how proud and thankful we (his parents and family) are of you and what you are trying to do to protect us all. This was Dan's second tour in Iraq – he knew and said that his being there was to protect us.

I want to encourage you. I hear in your speeches about "staying the course". I also know that many are against you in this "war on Terror" and that you must get weary in the fight to do what is right. We and many others are praying for you to see this through ---- as Lincoln said "that these might not have died in vain".

You have a heavy load – we are praying for you.

God bless you,

Bud Clay
6532 Terrasanta
Pensacola, FL 32504
850-791-6111

Author's Note: *This was Daniel Clay's last note to his family.*

Mom, Dad, Kristie, Jodie, Kimberly, Robert, Katy, Richard, and my Lisa:

Boy, do I love each and every one of you. This letter being read means that I have been deemed worthy of being with Christ, with Mama Jo, Mama Clay, Jennifer…all those we have been without for our time during the race. This is not a bad thing. It is what we hope for. The secret is out! He lives and His promises are real! It is not faith that supports this, but fact…and I am now a part of the promise. Here is notice! Wake up! All that we hope for is real. Not a hope. But real.

But here is something tangible. What we have done in Iraq is worth my sacrifice. Why? Because it was our duty. That sounds simple, but all of us have a duty. Duty is defined as a God-given task. Without duty, life is worthless. It offers no type of fulfillment. The simple fact that our bodies are built for work has to lead us to the conclusion that God (who made us) put us together to do His work. His work is different for each of us.

Mom, yours was to be the glue of our family, to be a pillar for those women (all women around you). Dad, yours was to train and build us (like a Platoon Sgt) to better serve Him. Kristie, Kim, Katy—you are the five team leaders who support your squad leaders, Jodie, Robert, and Richard. Lisa, you too. You are my XO and you did a hell of a job. You all have your duties. Be thankful that God in His wisdom gives us work. Mine was to ensure that you didn't have to experience what it takes to protect what we have as a family. This I am so thankful for. I know what honor is. It is not a word to be thrown around. It has been an honor to protect and serve all of you. I faced death with the secure knowledge that you would not have to. This is as close to Christlike as I can be. That emulation is where all honor lies. I thank you for making it worthwhile.

As a Marine, this is not the last chapter. I have the privilege of being one who has finished the race. I have been in the company of heroes. I now am counted among them. Never falter! Don't hesitate to honor and support those of us who have the honor of protecting that which is worth protecting.

Now, here are my final wishes. Do not cry! To do so is to not realize what we have placed all our hope and faith in. We should not fear. We should not be sad. Be thankful. Be so thankful. All we hoped for is true. Celebrate! My race is over, my time in war zone is over. My trials are done. A short time separates all of us from His reality. So laugh. Enjoy the moments and your duty. God is wonderful.

I love each and every one of you.

Spread the Word…Christ lives and He is real.

Semper Fidelis

Notes

Foreword

1. From an address by George C. Marshall, given in June 1941 at Trinity College, an Episcopalian institution in Hartford, Connecticut. Also included in *Selected Speeches and Statements of General of the Army George C. Marshall*, by H. A. deWeerd, ed. (*The Infantry Journal*, 1945), 121–25.

Chapter 3

2. Joseph H. Friend and David B. Guralnik, eds., *Webster's New World Dictionary* (New York: The World Publishing Co., 1953), 1094, s.v. "pestilence."

Chapter 5

3. Ronald Youngblood, ed., *Nelson's New Illustrated Bible Dictionary* (Nashville: Thomas Nelson, 1995), 231.
4. Katherine Pollard Carter, *The Mighty Hand of God* (Kirkwood, MO: Impact Christian Books, 1992), 31–32.

Chapter 11

5. Source unknown.

Chapter 12

6. C. S. Lewis, "Miracles," *God in the Dark* (Grand Rapids, MI: William B. eerdman's Publishers, 1970), 27–28.

Chapter 15

7. Story taken from Eddie Rickenbacker's autobiography.

Chapter 18

8. These words come from a poem called "Abide with Me." They were written by Henry Lyte, pastor at All Saints' Church in Lower Brixham, Devonshire, England, on the night before the author's farewell sermon in 1847. He passed away soon after from tuberculosis.

Chapter 20

9. Walter B. Knight, *Knight's Master Book of 4,000 Illustrations* (Grand Rapids, MI: William B. Eerdmans Publishing Company, 1981), 528.

Psalm 91 Testimonies

10. Matthew Seully, "True Value," taken from *The American Spectator* (Christianity Today International/Men of Integrity), used by permission.

11. Corrie ten boom, *Clippings From My Notebook* (Nashville, TN: Thomas Nelson Publishers, 1982) p. 41-42.

12. Peter K. Johnson, "Faith in Uniform," Charisma Magazine, October 2004.

About the Authors

 **Peggy Joyce Ruth** enjoys challenging people to move into a deeper understanding of the Word of God. While working alongside her husband, Jack, who pastored for thirty years, she has accumulated many exciting experiences. People came from all over to hear Peggy Joyce teach Tuesday morning ladies' Bible study, her popular Wednesday night adult Bible study, and yearly retreats and conferences.

She still teaches a weekly *Better Living* radio Bible program on two Christian radio stations. Some of her favorite experiences include teaching on a Caribbean Christian cruise ship, being elected as team cook for thirty-two Howard Payne University students on a mission trip into the Tenderloin area of San Francisco, and going with them again on a mission trip to the Philippines where she conducted a conference sponsored by twenty Filipino churches.

She followed up the next year with conferences all over the islands reaching into remote places where many have little access to the Word of God. She traveled to Germany recently to meet with chaplains stationed all over Germany.

Peggy Joyce Ruth has authored six books and has appeared on numerous television stations for interviews. She is a popular speaker for conferences because of her warm storytelling techniques, her easy-to-understand style of communicating the Word of God, and her pleasing sense of humor. Peggy Joyce speaks to soldiers who are being deployed from U.S. military bases and encourages them that God's Word offers promises for their exact situation. Workbooks are also available through Peggy Joyce Ruth Ministries for chaplains to take their soldiers through an in-depth study of Psalm 91.

Angelia Ruth Schum and her husband, Dr. David K. Schum, live in Brownwood, Texas. They have an adopted daughter, Jolena, married to Heath Adams, who is in the USAF and is stationed in Great Falls, Montana. David and Angelia operate a coffeehouse on the Howard Payne College campus and minister to students. Angelia manages two Christian Radio stations, KPSM 99.3FM and KBUB 90.3FM.

While in college Angie began a discipleship program that continues until today which trains college students to minister to incarcerated youth. That program has expanded its outreach to numerous prisons. Angie's message is that God has an exciting life for you!

Angelia had her first mission experience while smuggling Bibles with Donna Crow into the Underground Church in China, and wrote about this experience in the book *God's Smuggler, Jr.* She and her husband now take teams of college students to mission fields around the world, and Angelia has evangelized in more than thirty countries. She has ministered in leper colonies, TB hospitals, death row prisons, has been caught in the middle of riots, typhoons, and exploding live volcanoes, has eaten dog in the jungles, and has ridden camel-back down the Mount of Olives.

Her most memorable experiences include meeting with the pastor of the Underground Church in China and taking one of the few groups allowed into Ground Zero within weeks of the 9/11 bombing. In the summer of 2009 she and a college mission team spoke on Psalm 91 and handed out books to the underground church in Vietnam.

Angelia also has a passion for the military and has personally distributed books to U.S. chaplains in Germany, South Korea, and Mindanao. She speaks to the soldiers about the importance of Psalm 91 and tells of the undeniable connection this psalm has had with the military, from the Civil War to present times. She gives presentations in military chapels and to troops who are deploying, and distributes books to the soldiers in appreciation for their serving our country. She feels that this book is a story of soldiers speaking to soldiers and has shared many a tear with WWII veterans, as they have told their heart-wrenching stories of battle and POW imprisonment. Her gift for motivating is evident in the appeal she has for both young and old, and in encouraging soldiers to believe that God has exciting plans for their lives.

In her spare time, Angelia is working on her master's degree in youth ministry/theology.

To make donations, to submit Psalm 91 Testimonies, for author speaking engagements, or for information on other books available from these authors, please contact Better Living Ministries, which is a 501 (C) (3) corporation and is the umbrella corporation for Peggy Joyce Ruth Ministries, at (877) 972-6657. Or, on the Web at www.peggyjoyceruth.org.